D1357147

International Federation of Library Associations and Institutions
Fédération Internationale des Associations de Bibliothécaires et des Bibliothèques
Internationaler Verband der bibliothekarischen Vereine und Institutionen
Международная Федерация Библиотечных Ассоциаций и Учреждений
Federación Internacional de Asociaciones de Bibliotecarios y Bibliotecas

IFLA Publications 76

Measuring Quality

International Guidelines for Performance
Measurement in Academic Libraries

IFLA Section of University Libraries
& other General Research Libraries

Roswitha Poll and Peter te Boekhorst

in collaboration with
Ramon Abad Hiraldo, Aase Lindahl,
Rolf Schuursma, Gwenda Thomas,
and John Willemse

K · G · Saur
München · New Providence · London · Paris 1996

IFLA Publications
edited by Carol Henry

Recommended catalog entry:

Poll, Roswitha : Measuring quality : international guidelines for performance
measurement in academic libraries / Roswitha Poll and Peter te Boekhorst.
IFLA Section of University Libraries & Other General Research Libraries. In collab.
with Ramon Abad Hiraldo ... – München ; New Providence ; London ; Paris :
Saur, 1996, 171 p. 21 cm
   (IFLA publications ; 76)
   ISBN 3-598-21800-1

Die Deutsche Bibliothek – CIP-Einheitsaufnahme

Poll, Roswitha : Measuring quality : international guidelines for performance
measurement in academic libraries / Roswitha Poll and Peter te Boekhorst.
IFLA Section of University Libraries & Other General Research Libraries. In collab.
with Ramon Abad Hiraldo ... – München ; New Providence ; London ; Paris :
Saur, 1996
   (IFLA publications ; 76)
   ISBN 3-598-21800-1
NE: Boekhorst, Peter te:; International Federation of Library
   Associations and Institutions: IFLA publications

Printed on acid-free paper
The paper used in this publication meets the minimum requirements of American National
Standard for Information Sciences – Permanence of Paper for Printed Library Materials,
ANSI Z39.48.1984.

Druck / Printed by Strauss Offsetdruck GmbH, Mörlenbach
Binden / Bound by Buchbinderei Schaumann, Darmstadt
ISBN 3-598-21800-1
ISSN 0344-6891 (IFLA Publications)

Table of Contents

Performance Indicators

Glossaries

Selected Bibliography

The pretension is nothing; the performance every thing.
A good apple is better than an insipid peach.

Leigh Hunt

That action is best, which procures the greatest happiness
for the greatest numbers.

Francis Hutcheson

Measure thrice before you cut once.

Proverb

Preface

These guidelines have been drawn up by a working group of the IFLA Section of University Libraries and other General Research Libraries. Since 1988 the section has regarded performance measurement as a focal point of their work. At the IFLA conference in Sydney (1988) the theme was introduced in a paper of John Willemse. At the following conference in Paris (1989) the section organized a workshop on performance measures. The very lively workshop produced an initial list of interesting indicators:

➀ Relevance in collection development

➁ Degree of satisfaction

➂ Hours open

➃ Delay between order and availability on shelves

➄ Percentage of requested items obtained.

At the Stockholm conference (1990), the workshop was followed up by an open session on performance measures after which the IFLA section decided to establish a working group for guidelines of performance measurement. Members of the working group:

> Ramon Abad (Instituto Cervantes, New York)
> Peter te Boekhorst (Münster)
> Aase Lindahl (Odense)
> Roswitha Poll (Münster, chair)
> Rolf Schuursma (Rotterdam)
>
> Corresponding Members:
> Gwenda (Dalton)Thomas (Pretoria)
> John Willemse (Pretoria).

The group began to work in 1991 and decided on the following criteria which were approved by the IFLA section:

- To concentrate on academic libraries (according to the section)

- To include primarily indicators that would be applicable in all countries (developing as well as developed)

- To take care that the indicators should be applicable to all types of academic libraries, whether big or small, automated or not, with free access or closed stacks.

- To measure effectiveness, not efficiency (cost-effectiveness)

7

- To concentrate on user-orientated indicators (that excludes for example indicators for collection preservation)

- To include "overall" indicators (for example user satisfaction with the whole library) as well as indicators for separate activities.

The working group could only hope to obtain these goals by concentrating on a very limited number of indicators and by stressing the point that they must be easy to use, so that nobody would be kept from using the indicators for lack of mathematical or statistical knowledge.

After evaluating the existing literature on performance measurement, a list of about 30 indicators was chosen that was later on narrowed down to 17. It was deemed impossible to test all of those indicators in the libraries of the working group, but the group decided to apply as many indicators as possible with the help of other libraries in order to analyse problems and to see whether there ought to be alternative methods for an indicator. The libraries of several German polytechnics joined in those experiments.

A poster session at the annual conference in Moscow (1991) showed the first results. Although the poster session was timed at the first day of the putsch - the posters had to be carried over the barricades - the interest was enormous and the group was encouraged to go on with their concept. The next results were shown in a workshop at the New Delhi conference (1992), and a first draft of the guidelines was presented at the Barcelona conference (1993). The working group received numerous comments and suggestions, due also to a discussion group on performance measurement already established by the IFLA section. While these comments and the results of further practical tests of performance indicators were included in the guidelines, two members of the working group joined a new ISO group (TC 46/SC 8/WG 4), which was established to develop an international standard of library performance indicators. They brought the practical experience of the IFLA working group to the ISO discussion, whereas the standardization work influenced these guidelines.

Since the guidelines are aimed at "University and other General Research Libraries", the members of the IFLA section, the term "**academic library**" was chosen for the target group.

The guidelines describe one set of indicators, but are not regarded as a closed list. Academic libraries are changing, and new indicators might be added in the future. Nor is this list a must: Academic libraries all over the world show great varieties in organizational, financial, and technical conditions. Local circumstances will often make it necessary to modify the process of measuring, and not every indicator in the guidelines will apply to every library. Libraries should choose the indicators most useful to their next decisions; there is no need to apply them all. Measuring performance in only one sector will, however, be much less valid than combining several indicators or adding a questionnaire for user satisfaction to a quantified measure.

In most cases, it will be necessary to repeat the measuring process once or more in order to note changes and to see whether organizational steps after a first measurement have been effective.

Each indicator is meant to assess either the quality of the library's overall performance, or the quality of a specific activity or service. However, in some cases several aspects of library service have been combined in one indicator, out of the practical consideration of using one interview or questionnaire only. "Availability", for instance, tries to assess the quality of the collection, as well as the accuracy of catalogues and shelving. Most indicators are are suited to the data being split up in regards to

- types of users
- subject areas of the collection.

There are some things we could not hope to achieve in these guidelines:

- We do not presume to measure the outcome (impact) of library activities, i.e. the results of using the library for research. Though a few methods have been proposed in literature, we did not think them sufficiently valid.

- We have concentrated on effectiveness, not cost-effectiveness (efficiency). Because of the immense differences between budgetary and financial conditions for libraries in different countries, we could not hope to develop indicators suitable for all. Leaving out the cost factor may make the guidelines acceptable to librarians who are afraid of being evaluated on the scale of "how much circulation at the least cost". Nevertheless, we have added a short introduction to the theme of cost-effectiveness to the guidelines in order to show problems and possibilities.

- Measurement of performance, evaluation of library quality,requires a statement of what is thought to be "goodness" in each library. Performance can only be evaluated according to the goals of libraries. We have, therefore, tried to draw up a statement of what we consider to be the mission and the major goals of an academic library. Our choice of performance indicators is closely related to those goals. What we did not want to include in this book is a kind of recipe of:

  - How to state a mission
  - How to draw up a library plan
  - How to develop goals according to the mission statement.

We have included in the guidelines a rather comprehensive bibliography of literature dealing with performance measurement, because we thought it probable that many libraries do not possess all the handbooks and bibliographies already published on the topic.

For our work, we have, of course, consulted the wide range of existing literature on performance measurement, especially the reports on actual applications of indicators. Our reason for adding to the existing handbooks for performance measurement was that the handbooks have been either developed for public libraries, or stem from conditions in one country only. Another reason was that although several of the indicators proposed in the handbooks are useful operational data, we do not deem them to be indicators in the sense of valid statements about the level of performance.

The main goals of these guidelines are:

❶ To promote acceptance of performance measurement as an important tool for effective management

❷ To help get reliable results with a reasonable expenditure of work

❸ To offer tools for the evaluation process that, by using them in an identical way, allow historical comparisons within the library and even comparisons between libraries.

Measuring performance should not be equated with better performance; it is a means to that end.

Acknowledgements

The authors are grateful to all colleagues for their comments and suggestions which helped to improve the guidelines.

Special thanks are due to those libraries which took part in testing the indicators.

The authors would like to thank Anne Schuursma, Richard Parker, and the IFLA headquarters for proof-reading the text, but retain responsibility for all errors and omissions.

Thanks are due to the colleagues who helped with the translation of the glossary, especially Michel Netzer and Olga Azarova, and to Andreas Rafalski for a great part of the typewriting.

General Introduction

Today academic libraries all over the world recognize the need for effective management tools. This interest in management, that in some countries has become almost a routine while in others it is just beginning, has been brought about by changes that strongly affect the organizational structure of libraries:

- Academic libraries are carrying out more of their activities with the help of computers.

- World-wide, more and more information is offered as non-print material, especially in machine-readable form, and must be made accessible to the users.

- Resources are dwindling, and collections as well as organizational habits have to be adapted to the changing circumstances. It is necessary to find instruments for resource allocation.

- With less money for local collections, but more information available world-wide, the librarian's role changes from the administrator of collections to the mediator of information.

- Accountability of service institutions is of major interest to the administration.

- Public relations are becoming increasingly more important: Libraries need tools to demonstrate and publish their activities with.

In short: Libraries like other service institutions have to show that they are using given resources for the right purpose and in the best way, that they are providing high quality services.

Quality

If we say libraries should make use of effective quality management techniques, we need to know what we mean by quality.
The definition of quality has developed from the product-oriented aspect of control and inspection to a broader service-oriented concept that involves the whole organizational structure. Quality in this sense is fitness for purpose, that is to say, a service or product should supply or perform as it is intended to. The "purpose" of a service or product is defined by the customers. Quality in this sense is neither an isolated standard nor the highest standard; it is defined by the needs of the clientele of the individual institution. This is clearly stated in ISO 8402, where quality is defined as "the totality of features and characteristics of a product or service that

bear on its ability to satisfy stated or implied needs."[1]
This definition, including "implied needs", applies to libraries in a special way, as in addition to current demand they have to consider future requirements, for instance in coordinated collection building.

Quality Management

Managing quality comprises three steps:
- Quality planning
- Quality control
- Quality improvement[2]

or, very simply expressed, we must know
- what we want to do
- what we are already doing
- how we can improve on what we are doing.

For a library, managing service quality would mean something like this:

- To define the library's mission and primary user group
- To discover users' stated or implied needs
- To establish long-term goals and short-term objectives
- To design adequate services
- To deliver those services to the highest possible level
- To measure performance, and to compare performance and goals
- To implement a structure of continuous performance improvement
- To build up a climate of user orientation and service quality.

Two steps in this procedure are especially important: The definition of goals, and the control whether they have been achieved.

Mission and Goals

Since quality is fitness for purpose, the specific definition of quality for an individual library is determined by its own purpose or mission. Therefore, before committing itself to a standard of quality, each library needs to define its own mission and goals.

---

[1] ISO 8402: 1994, Quality Management and Quality Assurance - Vocabulary.

[2] J.M. Juran and F.M. Gryna: Quality Planning and Analysis: From Product Development through Use. - 3rd ed. - New York: McGraw Hill, 1993, pp. 3-9.

Stating the mission of the library means formally describing the framework within which the library is to move. The mission statement should specify the primary user group whom the library intends to serve and what kind of fundamental services are intended to be offered.

The mission of an academic library can be summarized as follows:

> To select, collect, organize and provide access to information for users, in the first place for the primary user group, namely the members of the institution.

Goals of the Academic Library[3]

Long-term goals can be developed from the mission statement. In order to accomplish the previously stated mission, the following goals must be achieved:

Collection:

- To provide all types of information, from print material and microfilms to audio-visual material, sound recordings, material in machine-readable form (software), etc.

  - according to the needs of the primary group and the special functions of the library
  - as promptly as possible
  - to the highest percentage possible (in terms of relevance to the users' needs).

Access:

- To inform the user about the existing collection by catalogues that are comprehensive, up-to-date, and easy to use, and which can be consulted by a number of users simultaneously

- To provide access to material preferably in open stacks as far as compliant with the preservation of materials

---

[3] The list partly relies on the following standards:

Standards for University Libraries: Evaluation of Performance /Prepared by ACRL's University Libraries Section's University Library Standards Review Committee, Kent Hendrickson, Chair (Approved June 1989). - Chicago: Association of College & Research Libraries, 1989.

Standards for College Libraries, 1995 Edition. Final Version Approved by the ACRL Board and the ALA Standards Committee, Diane C. Parker, Chair. - In: College and Research Library News, 56 (1995), 245-257.

- To ensure quick access to material in closed stacks

- To provide opening hours that are consistent with reasonable demand

- To provide free access without charging fees for the main services of the library

- To ensure services within easy reach of the primary user group and with good access for handicapped persons

- To quickly provide access to material that is not in the own collection but available elsewhere.

In-house Use:

- To provide adequate space and facilities for study and research in the library

- To provide adequate equipment for the use of non-print material.

User Education:

- To inform the public about the services of the library

- To assist the users in finding the information they want inside and outside the library by instruction and personal interaction

- To provide adequate reference services in printed as well as in electronic form.

Storage and Preservation:

- To store the acquired material as long as it is relevant to research work in the institution or to other functions (e.g., special collections) of the library

- To provide safe and adequate housing for all material

- To take care of the preservation and conservation of rare materials.

In order to reach these goals, academic libraries

- apply their resources in a cost-effective way and use new management techniques

- adopt - as far as possible - useful new technologies

- take part in co-operative programmes in oder to enhance the collection of the library and the range of services

- enable their staff to acquire the necessary knowledge of new information material and techniques.

Of course, many academic libraries have special tasks that would involve other goals to be added to this list. Special functions that often occur in academic libaries could be for instance:

- Legal deposit collections
- Functions in national collection plans
- Function as training centre.

According to its goals, a library should draw up a plan of objectives (short-term goals) for the separate activities. Usually this is done first. The many special objectives must also fit into the long-term planning. Such objectives should be realistic, achievable within a given deadline. They should also be agreed upon by the library as well as its stakeholders. The results should be measurable.

If the goal is for instance to inform the user by comprehensive and up-to-date catalogues, the objectives might be

- to eliminate backlogs within a certain time
- to include material described in a separate catalogue in the general catalogue.

Concrete objectives for the next two or three years will of course depend very much on the amount of resources the library can hope to receive. Some libraries have negotiated with their parent institution for the service quality to be maintained or achieved within a certain time and the amount of resources this would require. Such "service level agreements" can help the library to obtain additional funds for clearly defined tasks, as the funding institution can always control whether it gets value for money.[4]

Stakeholder Approach

Mission, goals and objectives must meet the interests of the customer. Quality management in recent years has attached a broader meaning to what constitutes the "customers", namely all

---

[4] See Geoffrey Ford: Service Level Agreements - Vereinbarungen über das Dienstleistungsniveau. - In: Zeitschrift für Bibliothekswesen und Bibliographie, 43 (1996).

"stakeholders" of interests.[5] For an academic library, this could include:

- The primary user group (members of the institution)
- Other users
- Library staff
- The managers of the institution
- All resource allocators
- Government
- The research community outside the institution
- Cooperating libraries
- And even society in the broadest sense, including posterity.

This comprehensive approach requires that the defining of the mission, goals and objectives is not the sole responsibility of the library, but that users, staff, the institution's management and resource allocators are to be included in that definition process. The mission, goals, and objectives should also take in consideration:

- General political targets
- The interests of the research community as represented in the cooperation of libraries
- As far as possible, predictable future demands.

Performance Measurement

Quality planning must be followed by quality control. A measuring instrument is needed to indicate whether a library is coming up to its planning. Such an instrument is performance measurement.

Performance measurement means collection of statistical and other data describing the performance of the library, and the analysis of these data in order to evaluate the performance. Or, in other words: Comparing what a library is doing (performance) with what it is meant to do (mission) and wants to achieve (goals).

Performance is the degree to which a library is achieving its objectives, particularly in terms of users' needs.

A *performance indicator* (as we use the term in these guidelines) is a quantified statement used to evaluate and compare the performance of a library in achieving its objectives.[6]

---

[5] Peter Brophy: Quality Management in Libraries. - In: Proceedings of the 1st Northumbria International Conference on Performance Measurement in Libraries and Information Services / Editor Pat Wressell. - Newcastle upon Tyne: Information North, 1995, p. 77. See also Peter Brophy and Kate Coulling: Quality Management for Information and Library Managers. - Aldershot: Aslib Gower, 1996, pp. 40-41.

[6] The terms "performance measure" or "output measure" have often been used in the same sense. "Indicator" has also been used as a combination of simpler "measures".

Comparing results of performance measurement with goals and objectives will not only result in organizational measures for better performance, but will often lead to re-formulation and specification of goals and objectives. The results of performance measurement will show if goals have been fixed too high (unobtainable) or too low (easily surpassed). Measuring use and user satisfaction will show whether users' needs have altered and whether goals need to be re-defined. Planning, measuring, and improving are a continuous process.

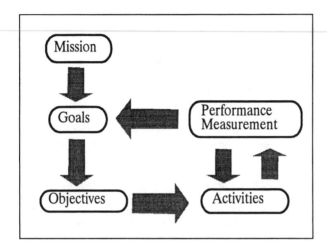

Statistics and Performance Measurement

Most academic libraries regularly collect statistical data of their resources and output. Many countries have national library statistics, some are even very detailed and well-defined. Collecting data regularly provides a useful basis for performance measurement. But the existing statistics differ from performance measurement as follows:

- Library statistics concentrate on positive data: They note circulations, users, volumes, or opening hours. They do not ask for the non-user, the part of the collection not used, or the volumes missed on the shelves.

- Statistics are regularly collected in areas where it is easy to get exact data: resources (staff, funds, collection), outputs (circulation, questions answered). Performance measurement asks for additional data that are more difficult to obtain: Is there sufficient staff at the reference desk? Did the users get relevant answers? Is the collection built up according to the needs of the users?

17

- Performance measurement compares the data and combines them:

  - Circulation per group of undergraduates
  - Circulation of a subject collection compared to acquisition (funds, volumes) in that same area.

- Performance measurement adds "subjective" data, especially users' opinion on services, to "objective" data.

- Performance measurement relates the data to the goals of the library.

Criteria for a Performance Indicator

An often cited description of what constitutes a performance indicator was given by Orr in 1973.[7] A performance indicator should be appropriate, informative, valid, reproducible, and practical, fit for being used for comparative purposes. These criteria still show the most important points.

- A performance indicator should be *appropriate* (valid) for what it is supposed to measure. This is a very important point. A performance indicator is applied in order to answer a particular question, and the results should provide this answer.

- It should be *reliable* (accurate). That means, it should be devoid of ambiguity. This is an ideal demand which will not always be fulfilled, e.g. where performance indicators try to analyse an attitude or opinion, the results of which cannot be numeric.

- It should be *reproducible*; the same things should always be counted or measured in the same way. To achieve this, the separate steps of the indicator should be exactly described, and the activities, persons or things measured precisely defined.

  In this way, performance measurement will allow comparison

  - of performance in the same library at different times

---

[7] R. H. Orr: Measuring the Goodness of Library Services: A General Framework for Considering Quantitative Measures. - In: Journal of Documentation, 29 (1973), p. 315-332.

- between libraries of a similar type.

● It should be *helpful* (useful, informative) in decision-making.
  - It should show causes of failure and short-comings, e.g.:
    - Users' lack of the necessary skills
    - Resources not applied at the crucial points
    - Defects in the library's work-flow.
  - It should show the users' needs.
  - It should help to find ways for obtaining better performance.

  Summarized: It should not only show what is happening, but allow interpretation of quality, failure and ways of improvement.
  To achieve all this, the indicator must be related to the goals of the library.

● A performance indicator should be *practical* (user friendly). This will, of course, further its acceptance, but it is doubtful whether this ought to be regarded as an indispensable criterion. If a library is especially interested in gaining information on a certain question, even a more lengthy and complicated procedure of evaluation might be acceptable. In any case, a complicated indicator can be reliable, reproducible, appropriate and helpful.

Difficulties

The results of a performance measurement ought to be reliable and comparable. But even where seemingly "objective" data are collected, each project requires exact definitions of the sample, the time of measuring, and the activities or objects to be measured. One example can show this:

Opening hours:
- Needs to be defined, whether this only means access to the reading-room, or access to the major services
- Needs to differentiate between normal opening hours and reduced times, e.g. during vacation periods
- If there are several libraries in the institution, or if the library is divided up into several buildings with different opening times, the "regular" opening hours have to be defined.

Performance measurement tries to ascertain not only users' needs, but also the users' opinion of the library's services and facilities. This is done by "user satisfaction surveys", questionnaires and interviews asking for satisfaction with the library or with special activities.

19

The users' comments (whether given in an interview or on a questionnaire) can be influenced by many circumstances:

- The users' experience of libraries up to that time period. If they have never experienced better possibilities, the library might get quite a good satisfaction rate without a good service. On the other side, user expectation might be too high compared to bigger, better financed libraries.

- The time the survey is taken can bias the opinion. At the beginning of the term, when many new users visit the library, wishes might be different from those at other times.

- The formulation of the questions must be carefully considered, as it will easily influence the scope of answers.

Results of a user satisfaction survey cannot be, for instance, as reliable as data of book processing time, but they give additional information that cannot be gained in any other way. It has proved extremely useful to follow up the issues mentioned in a user satisfaction survey by more "objective" indicators in order to confirm or explain the results. For example: If users complain about the library's collection being incomplete, measuring the availability of required titles in the collection will show whether the complaints are well-founded or biased by some few bad experiences.

Measuring Outcome

Since performance is meant to match goals, especially in regards to users' needs, it is obvious that measuring performance is a difficult process. Users are "multi-goaled individuals, who have immediate goals which are generally different each time they approach the library."[8] Users' needs as well as library goals cannot be stated in figures and will always be changing. In measuring performance, the ideal would be to measure *outcome* or impact: the effect of the library's services on the user. For academic libraries this would mean: the effects on the quality and quantity of research and training. Only a few methods have been proposed that aim directly to measure this. One example is "document exposure"[9]: Users were asked to note down the time they "exposed" themselves to a book and to state whether they had derived any benefit from it. Some studies, mostly done in Australia, have tried to assess a relationship between library use and persistence in studies,[10] or library use and academic success of students.[11]

---

[8] Betty Sell: An Evaluative, Holistic and User-orientated Approach to Assessing and Monitoring Effectiveness of the Academic Library in Its Setting. - In: Library Effectiveness - A State of the Art. - New York, 1980, p. 297.

[9] Don H. Revill: Performance Measures for Academic Libraries.-In: Encyclopedia of Library and Information Science / Ed. Allen Kent. - Vol. 45, Supplement 10. - New York: Dekker, 1990, p. 327.

[10] Lloyd A. Kramer and Martha B. Kramer: The College Library and the Drop-Out. - In: College and Research Libraries, 29 (1968), pp. 310-312.

Others have tried to relate the quantity of published work produced by the university staff with their use of the library. But as one cannot separate knowledge derived from library use from that from other sources, it seems impossible to arrive at a valid measure for outcome.

Therefore, performance measurement tries a less direct way by choosing "indicators" that seem to represent the impact of library services on the user. If for instance we calculate the percentage of the primary user group visiting the library at least once a year, we imply that they will benefit from a library visit. Or if we count the successful searches in the author catalogue, we suppose that the material found will be useful to the user.

Results of Performance Measurement

When interpreting performance measurement one must always consider that

- a single application of an indicator only shows the situation at a certain time; it might be necessary to repeat it to gain valid information.

- in most cases the indicators evaluate only one activity of the library; using several indicators would give a more reliable and detailed picture of the performance of a service (e.g. collection use and availability used together).

- using a performance indicator can show low or high performance, but additional investigation will often be necessary to find the causes.

If not over-interpreted, performance measurement will allow useful information to enhance the quality of services:

- It shows the present-day state of performance
- It enables the library to compare variations in performance over the years
- It helps to identify causes of low performance.

The results can suggest changes in management such as altering the work-flow and setting new priorities in the allocation of resources.

---

[11] Jane E. Hiscock: Does Library Usage affect Academic Performance? - In: Australian Academic and Research Libraries, 17 (1986), pp. 207-213; Karin de Jager: Library Use and Academic Achievement. - In: Proceedings of the 1st Northumbria International Conference on Performance Measurement in Libraries and Information Services / Edited Pat Wressell. - Newcastle upon Tyne: Information North, 1995, p. 287; James Self: Reserve Readings and Student Grades: Analysis of a Case Study. - In: Library and Information Science Research, 9 (1987), pp. 29-40; J. Wells: The Influence of Library Usage on Undergraduate Academic Success. - In: Australian Academic and Research Libraries, 26 (1995), pp. 121-128.

Beside this internal evaluation, which is, of course, most important to libraries, performance measurement can also be used for external purposes:

- To justify expenses and show results
- To inform the users and potential users about the library's activities and services
- To inform the authorities about possible consequences of augmented or diminished resources.

If a library uses indicators that have been tested and generally approved, comparison with other libraries (benchmarking) may also be possible on condition that

- the libraries have a similar mission and structure
- and that the indicator has been used in the same - or nearly the same - circumstances.

The interests of an administration will, of course, not be restricted to the degree of performance, but will extend to the question of costs. Though indicators for measuring efficiency have not been included in these guidelines, the question is so vital for libraries that a chapter on cost-effectiveness has been added in order to give some general indication of how to deal with this question.

The Measurement Process

It is the exception rather than the rule that libraries will apply systematically all measures described in a handbook of performance measurement.[12] Rather, the library will be interested in obtaining better knowledge about one or several specific services or activities. The library becomes aware of the organizational necessity to improve special aspects of library services, because

- users complain about bad service, e.g. insufficient opening hours or unsatisfactory availability ratios

- members of staff make suggestions how a particular service might be improved

- traditional controlling mechanisms like library statistics point to diminishing outputs in certain areas

- the organizational structure is changed, e.g. by introducing new technologies which alter established procedures

- other libraries lead the way by streamlining organizational procedures in certain fields.

When the library has clearly stated what sort of results it wants to obtain from the measurement, the next step will be the choice of an indicator. There are often several indicators possible for measuring a certain activity, all of which have been tested and found to be appropriate, reliable, reproducible, helpful and practical. The choice then depends on the following aspects:

- The better the indicator matches the problem the better the results. A user satisfaction survey will help to understand the users' complaints that they do not get the books they are looking for. A study of the collection use will elucidate the problem. It is, however, the availability study that indicates points of departure from which to tackle the complaints.

- The application of the indicator should lead to tangible results within a short period of time.

---

[12] The ALA-handbook "Measuring Academic Library Performance - A Practical Approach" was tested and evaluated at Stockholm University Library. See Törngren, Margareta et al.: RUT: Resultatmätning och utvärdering av mätmetoder: Test och utvärdering av handboken Measuring Academic Library Performance - A Practical Approach samt resultat av mätningar vid Stockholms universitetsbibliotek. Stockholm: Kungl. Biblioteket, 1993 (BIBSAM-Sekretariat för nationell planering och samordning ; report nr. 6).

- The decision also depends on cost-benefit considerations. Some of the measures, especially if conducted for the first time, are very labour-intensive and time-consuming. Unless the library is vitally interested in certain results, it should think twice before starting on such a venture. In these regards it is important to state which of the data that are necessary for the measurement are already available or can be obtained easily. If, for instance, either acquisition speed or book processing speed is to be examined, a decision might depend on the fact that for the latter the data are easier obtainable whereas the former relies on data provided by the publishers.

Careful consideration of all these aspects will help the library to decide which performance indicator to choose. Once the choice has been made, the measurement process can begin.

- Each description of a performance indicator, apart from defining what is measured, includes sections on how the data are gathered and how they are calculated. Only reliable data allow for comparisons of measurements carried out at regular intervals within a single library as well as interlibrary comparisons.

- Each description aims at bridging the gap between simplicity and the demand for statistical accurateness. A librarian is not necessarily an experienced statistician who knows how to calculate sample sizes or confidence intervals. Those who regard the described methodology as too complicated should make use of the abundance of books on statistics and research methods.[13] Those librarians well-versed in the art of statistics are called upon to refine the methods wherever they regard it necessary.

The measurement process usually consists of three stages: preparation, realization, and interpretation.

Preparation: The responsibility for the whole project should lie in the hands of a supervisor. Apart from being familiar with both the measurement method and the organization of the library, he or she should function as a kind of clearing agency for all the problems arising throughout the measurement process.

---

[13] See, for example, Charles H. Busha, Stephen P. Harter: Research Methods in Librarianship: Techniques and Interpretation. - New York: Academic Press, 1980; John Martin, F. Wilfrid Lancaster: Investigative Methods in Library and Information Science: An Introduction. - Arlington, Va.: Information Resources Press, 1981; Ronald R. Powell: Basic Research Methods for Librarians. - Norwood, N.J.: Ablex, 1985; or Peter Stephen, Susan Hornby: Simple Statistics for Library and Information Professionals. - London: Library Association, 1995.

Right from the beginning staff members should be involved in each measurement project. It is very important to discuss the project with those persons who are actually responsible for the library service under surveillance. The library management should explain all aspects which lead to the decision to launch an evaluation project, and state its willingness to provide the necessary resources in terms of time and money; especially the reasons why a service needs improvement should be outlined. It is also necessary to state the expected gains for the library and its users. The staff will use the opportunity to suggest improvements and possible ways to achieve them. This exchange will positively influence the evaluation process. Furthermore, knowing best what to measure and how, the staff can help adapt the research method to the specific circumstances of the library. Staff involvement is also necessary to overcome the fear, that is now and then wrongly associated with performance measurement, namely the fear of having one's personal performance scrutinized.

Working Plan: Having outlined the aims and objectives as well as the expected outcome, a working plan is devised to estimate the necessary effort of the library. Here the cost-benefit considerations, which influenced the choice of a performance indicator, are put into more concrete terms:

- The time needed
- The number of staff members involved
- The material to be provided (e.g. questionnaires).

The performance indicator probably makes use of statistical data that are already known from annual statistics or that can be easily obtained from an automated library system. Each stage of the measurement process should be analysed. A flow chart might help to streamline the whole procedure.

Sampling: Statistical data are not always available, and in most cases it is too expensive to achieve a complete coverage. Therefore, sampling is very important. A small proportion of the total population is selected and the findings generalized to the larger group.

For most performance indicators an ideal sample size is recommended which can be considered as a rule of thumb based on practical experience and which will provide reliable results. Although it is true that the larger the sample the more reliable the results, the idea of sampling is to balance the desire for a maximum of reliable information with the necessity of a minimum of effort. Because of specific circumstances it might be necessary to calculate the sample size.

To calculate the sample size needed (n) it is best to use a probability sampling technique. This procedure is one in which each unit in the population has a known and non-zero probability of being included in the sample.

Before calculating the sample needed (n), certain decisions must be made, namely:

What will be the accuracy level (h)?

Where h = accuracy level (sampling error).
There are three "levels", namely:

"ball-park" accuracy only   -->   (h ≈ 0.10)
moderately high accuracy   -->   (h ≈ 0.03)
very high accuracy   -->   (h ≈ 0.01)

For use in a library, an accuracy level of 0.03
is suggested.

What will be the confidence level ($Z\alpha$)?

Where $z\alpha$ = "desired" confidence level e.g.

95% --> $Z\alpha$ = 1.960
90% --> $Z\alpha$ = 1.645

For the use in a library a confidence level of
95% is suggested.

What is the given planning proportion (p)?

where p = "use rate" or "success rate"
(NB: p is a fraction between 0 and 1).
A "success rate" of 61% is stated as p = 0.61.

Although the sample size will vary with the survey population and the predetermined accuracy and specified confidence levels, the basic formula used for calculating a sample size (n) is given by the formula:

$$n = \frac{Z\alpha^2 p(1-p)}{h^2 + \dfrac{Z\alpha^2 p(1-p)}{N}}$$

If the total population size (N) is large, i.e. more than about 20 times the sample size (i.e. (n) divided by (N) less than 0.05), then use the simplified formula:

26

$$n = \frac{Z\alpha^2 p(1-p)}{h^2}$$

Glossary of symbols:

$\approx$ is approximately equal to (e.g. $1.9999 \approx 2$)
$<$ is less than (e.g. $6 < 7$)
∞ infinite
x^2 read x^2 as x squared (e.g. $3^2 = 3 \times 3 = 9$)
N   number of units (measurements) in the population
n   number of units (measurements) in a sample

Example: A large library (assume $N = \infty$) believes that the availability of its ILL titles is about 80% (i.e. p = 0,8). Calculate the sample size (n) needed to achieve a moderately high accuracy (h = 0,03) for the availability (p). The result must be stated at the 95% confidence level ($Z\alpha$ = 1,960). (Hint: use simplified formula, because $N = \infty$).

Solution:

$$n = \frac{(1.960)^2 \times (0.8) \times (1 - 0.8)}{(0.03)^2}$$

$$n = \frac{3.8416 \times 0.8 \times 0.2}{0.0009}$$

$$n = \frac{0.614656}{0.0009}$$

$$n = 682.95111$$

$$\therefore n \approx 683$$

(A library handling 1200 ILL requests per year and the same success rate of 80% assumed will need a sample size of 435 items to secure a moderately high accuracy level [h = 0,03] and a 95% confidence level).

Stratified Sample: Keep in mind that a simple random sample ensures a random but not necessarily a representative sample. When the population is heterogeneous and can be divided into subgroups (called strata), e.g. local and international libraries, it is often better to use a stratified random sample.

NB: The number of units in the population and in each stratum should be known.

To calculate a stratified sample with proportional allocation, the following formula is given:

$$n_i = \frac{n}{N} \, N_i$$

Example: A large academic library requested during 1992 a total of 15,187 ILL items (N = 15187); 11,322 items from local libraries (N_i = 11322) and 3,865 items internationally (N_j = 3865). What will be the sample sizes for stratified sampling with proportional allocation for a survey in 1993?

$$n_i = \frac{n}{N} \, N_i \qquad\qquad n_j = \frac{n}{N} \, N_j$$

$$= \frac{683}{15187} \, (11322) \qquad\qquad = \frac{683}{15187} \, (3865)$$

$$\therefore n_i \approx 509 \qquad\qquad\qquad \therefore n_j \approx 174$$

Apart from the size of the sample, its design is of crucial importance. It depends on the special circumstances of the library. Usually, systematic and random sampling techniques have been used. Where special parts of an entire set of data are deliberately excluded as, for example, the journals or acquisitions by gift or exchange for the performance indicator "Subject Collection Use", this has to be stated explicitly. Knowing the overall number of units (e.g. 1,000) as well as the desired sample size (200), one has to analyse every fifth unit in the population, starting from a random number. When conducting a general library survey, every participant should be asked for information about his status (undergraduate, teaching staff, etc.). The results have to be interpreted in the light of this information about the composition of the population.

Another important issue is the data collection period. For financial and organizational reasons it is impossible to collect the data continuously. A sample period must be chosen providing representative data. Variations throughout the academic year should not influence the results too heavily. Usually the collection procedure should not exceed one week at a time. Concentrated efforts of data collection prevent users from getting bored by being asked to help the library improve its services.

Pretest: Before one can actually start gathering the data, it is necessary to conduct a pretest. Although design and methodology are described in detail for each indicator, the data gathering must be adapted to the particular circumstances of each library. Generally, pretests help avoid mistakes that might influence the validity of the results of the whole measurement effort:

- Wrong or incomplete description of procedures
- Faulty assumptions of how the user will behave
- Too high/low expectations of the user's skills.

Realization: The second part of the measurement process consists of collecting the data. In a few cases one can fall back on data that are collected continuously. To determine the market penetration, the governing body of the institution will, of course, provide the most recent figures for the number of students or members of teaching staff for each faculty or subject. In the case of collection use, the library itself has most of the important records for the number of loans per book according to the circulation record or the amount of books not used within a certain period of time. Quite a number of data are easily obtained. Yet, these data must be interpreted carefully in the context of the evaluation. Their use may be restricted because of data protection, or the data might have been collected for purposes differing from that of the evaluation; they even might be incomplete or out-dated.

Data Collection: In most cases the data have to be collected especially for the purpose of performance measurement. Among the numerous collection techniques,[14] four are of special importance for the practical application of performance indicators in the context of these guidelines:

❶ Simulation

❷ Interview

❸ Observation

❹ Survey/questionnaire.

Simulation: In order to spare the user the embarrassment of having his library skills examined for the indicator "Document Delivery Time", testees are selected who simulate the whole procedure of looking titles up and borrowing them. An actual user would see no reason to waste his time looking for a book he himself is not interested in. Simulation is also necessary because the sample of books must be chosen in advance to make sure that it is actually on the shelf. The choice of people to be used as simulators is very important, because it determines the success of the indicators as a whole. It is evident that trained librarians can be expected to be much more successful when tracing titles in the catalogue than undergraduates. Simulation is also used for the indicator "Correct Answer Fill Rate". Reference Questions which have previously been tested are asked at the reference desk by surrogate users.

Interview: In the context of the guidelines the interview technique, which is rather time-consuming and expensive, is used only for the performance indicator "Subject Search". In order to evaluate the search in an alphabetical or classified subject catalogue, the user first has to fill in a questionnaire and then is interviewed about the search strategy and its estimated success. Each interview should be preceded by a short explanation of what the library wants to achieve by this project.

---

[14] See also Peter Hernon, Charles R. McClure: Evaluation and Library Decision Making. - Norwood, NJ: Ablex, 1990, pp. 88-94; David Bawden: User-oriented Evaluation of Information Systems and Services. - Aldershot: Gower, 1990, pp. 27-63.

Telephone interviews can be used for the performance indicator "Market Penetration". Instead of mailing the questionnaire to members of the primary user group, the people in the sample could be contacted via telephone. Although this method excludes those who do not have telephones, it has the advantage of higher response rates because of the personal contact.

Observation: Observing the behaviour of users is a widely used data collection technique used in various forms ranging from self-observation, where users are asked to keep diaries about their behaviour, to participant observation, where observer and observed communicate with each other. What makes observation such an important method is the fact that users' skill can be examined under "real life" conditions.

For the performance indicator "Subject Search", a special variety of observation is used, namely unobtrusive observation. This form of observation leaves the user unaware of the staff member who tries to keep track of what the user is doing at the catalogue. This technique asks for a lot of sensitivity on the part of the staff member. As soon as the user notices that he/she is being observed, the whole procedure is spoiled, since the awareness of being observed changes the usual search behaviour.

A special form of unobtrusive observation is online monitoring or transaction log analysis, recording a user's complete session at an online public access catalogue. The advantages of this method are genuineness of results, preciseness of information, completeness of coverage, scope of analysis and efficiency in obtaining the data. Depending on legal regulations there might be problems because of privacy protection.

Survey/Questionnaire: By far the most important method of performance measurement is the survey. Most performance indicators are, at least partly, based on information directly obtained from the user. Despite the intricacies of questionnaire design,[15] sampling technique, and validity, the survey is the best method to evaluate library services since it facilitates the collection of large amounts of data in a relatively short period of time. Such a survey

- provides detailed information about the user's opinion of the service
- helps to clarify the librarian's concept of the service as well as his/her assumptions about the user's needs
- indicates problems
- suggests solutions.

The pretest is an indispensable means of refining questionnaires. The draft of the questionnaire should be shown to other experts as well as a group of users to find out poorly phrased and therefore ambiguous questions. Library jargon should be avoided wherever possible. Questions should be simple and to the point. Especially in the case of open-ended questions, users should be asked to give an account of "critical incidents", which he/she clearly remembers, rather than general opinions. Other factors influencing the success of a questionnaire are poor instructions or missing respectively superfluous questions.

---

[15] For a concise description of questionnaire design see Anne Russel, Michael Shoolbred: Developing an Effective Questionnaire. - In: Library and Information Research News, 19 (1995), pp. 28 - 33.

Surveys can ask for facts concerning the use of a service (e.g. indictor no. 7 "Known-Item-Search") or for the user's satisfaction with a service. User satisfaction surveys are based on short questionnaires consisting of a few central questions about a particular service. Usually, the user is asked to state his opinion by choosing one answer out of a five point Likert scale, ranging from e.g. very unsatisfactory to very satisfactory. It is, of course, a considerable disadvantage pressing the attitude of the user into the Procrustean bed of summated scales by restricting the responses of the participant to stated alternatives. Subtle distinctions between attitudes are thereby disregarded. Representing an ordinal scale of measurement, these scales do not permit pinpointing the exact amount of difference between the attitudes. These drawbacks are outweighed by the advantage of obtaining fixed, reliable answers. Open-ended questions might be more accurate in mirroring the user's opinion, but the answers are difficult to structure and quantify. Furthermore, structured questions can easily be precoded. Assigning fixed values to each answer facilitates the subsequent analysis of the data.

There are several distribution techniques. The highest response rate will be achieved if users are asked in a friendly way by members of the library staff to participate in a project to improve library services. Reluctant users will be persuaded more easily as soon as they know more about the purpose of the study. Leaving out a personal approach of the users by putting up signs informing them about the purpose of the evaluation and asking users to pick a questionnaire from a pile, has major disadvantages:

- Particularly users will participate who have a preconceived opinion of the library and its services and do not belong to the "silent majority".
- The overall response rate will be low.

In the case of mail questionnaires the response rate will also be low, even if it is accompanied by a cover letter, a self-addressed, stamped, return envelope and follow-up mailings.

Interpretation: The analysis and interpretation of the collected data is the final stage of the measurement process. The effort in calculating the results varies considerably. For the performance indicator "Expert Checklist", the title fill rate as percentage of titles in the list or biography that are in the collection, is easily calculated. More complicated is the calculation of 95% confidence intervals as described for the performance indicator "Availability", or the analysis of the results of a user satisfaction survey. If the librarian transcribes the observations or scores for each individual or case as numerical codes from the data collection instrument to a coding sheet, a computer is most useful. There are a lot of statistical software as well as spreadsheet packages on the market which cover basic calculating routines as well as aspects of descriptive statistics such as average, standard deviation, or confidence intervals.

The final results of the measurement process should be published in the library in order to raise comments from the staff. The performance measurement supervisor should discuss them in detail with the staff concerned. Central questions are:

What did we expect?
What do the figures tell us?
What are we going to do?

The last question is an especially difficult one, since a clear-cut correlation between cause and effect is the exception rather than the rule. The reasons for the user's failure may be manifold, ranging from lacking knowledge of library procedures to insufficient support or illegible catalogue cards. Even if the reason for a low performance in a certain field is clearly discernable, the library management might hesitate changing present procedures if it entails higher costs or more staff. In these circumstances a repetition of the measurement process at regular intervals is necessary to prove that the additional effort is justified. Repeated data collection improves the reliability of the data; it helps to decide whether the differences between the figures must be attributed to sample errors or interpreted as decisive change in the quality of a service.

Results: It is of crucial importance that the results of the measurement effort find their way into the working procedures of the library. The members of the staff must recognize the success of this effort in their everyday work in order to realise that performance measurement is neither an academic exercise nor a deliberate control mechanism, but leads to a qualitative improvement of library services.

The staff members must be informed about the results. A short summary illustrated with diagrams and stating the conclusions drawn from the project will be of interest to all members of the staff, even if they were not directly affected by the measure. This will also help to overcome possible resistance against performance measurement.

Results must be presented to the wider public. Especially the users who have actively taken part in the study have a right to know the outcome. This should even be done if the results are worse than expected. In that case special emphasis should be placed on the initiatives to improve the situation. If the results are good, presentation of the outcome is an effective public relations tool for the library as well as its governing body. It may even help the library to raise money for further improvement projects or for keeping high quality standards.

Systematic Performance Measurement: In the past, performance measurement has been mainly used to improve individual library services quickly. Interest in a more systematic application is the result of the growing importance of quality management in library and information services, which is inextricably bound up with the idea of continuous performance improvement. The so-called decision support system (DSS) has been developed as a tool for systematic measurement. A DSS can be defined as an "interactive computer-based information system containing databases and sets of rules".[16] It is designed to help the library management in its process of decision-making:

- Controlling the flood of operational data
- Providing current performance data
- Controlling the quality of library services
- Improving the effectiveness of the library
- Improving the efficiency of the library.

---

[16] Roy Adams: Decision Support Systems and Performance Assessment in Academic Libraries. - London: Bowker/Saur, 1993, p. 85.

At the core of every DSS is a set of performance indicators that is provided with the necessary data by either the automated library system or by manually conducted data collection procedures. These data have to be gathered continuously if the DSS is to fulfil its purpose of enhancing decision-making by replacing various rules of thumb with reliable operational data. Especially in the interest of more cost-effectiveness this systematic approach towards performance measurement will make DSS an attractive management tool for libraries.

Cost-effectiveness

Introduction: We have already explained that we offer international guidelines for measuring the quality of an academic library from the point of view of the user. In other words: measuring how effective the library is in offering services. Effectiveness, however, does not necessarily correlate with cost-effectiveness. An academic library which, in the view of its users, reaches a high degree of quality may, nonetheless, use its resources in a rather ineffective way.

Matters of cost and cost-effectiveness are, however, closely related to national or local financial structures. Because of the immense differences between budgetary and financial conditions for libraries in different countries, these guidelines refrain from providing indicators of cost-effectiveness.

This does not alter the fact that questions of cost and cost-effectiveness of library services are as important as measuring the user's satisfaction with those services. If library management is not posing such questions, they will certainly be posed by the financiers of the academic library. In many cases the answers given will have an immediate impact on the resources put at management's disposal. Therefore, this chapter discusses some principles of measuring cost-effectiveness and of its implementation within the parameters of each individual situation.

Resources/Allocations: Before measuring cost-effectiveness, the management of an academic library should first determine

- the resources available to the library

- the allocation of these resources to the different areas of the library's staff and material goods

- the input from these areas into the major services provided by the library.

In an academic library the resources will basically stem from a combination of the following (or part of the following) revenues:

- Funds allocated annually to the library by a university or research institution served by the library, or by a local or national government

- Donations from private persons or institutions

- Revenues from entrance charges, borrower's tickets, overdue fines, etc.

One should, of course, take into account that available resources can strongly differ from year to year. This is the more true since academic libraries are seldom financed according to their needs as stated in their long-range planning. Their income is greatly dependent on sometimes more or less random allocations by governing bodies which have to divide scarce funds over many institutions. Therefore, the measurement of the library's cost-effectiveness in a certain year should be related to the library's resources in that same year.

The library's resources will be allocated to various areas of the library's staff and material goods:

- The library's staff
- Its collection(s)
- Its networking
- Its capital goods such as building, furniture, and equipment.

The costs involved with these allocations will be accounted for per annum. This method should also be applied to capital goods which are paid for in one year, but which in many cases will be in use over several years. Dependent on the depreciation policy of the library or the institution the library is part of, the purchase price can be divided by as many years as the goods are supposed to last, after the estimated rest-value of the goods, if relevant, has been subtracted from the purchase price. The resulting per annum amount is comparable with the costs of staff, etc., during a certain year.

In order to make the measurements reasonably accurate, it is necessary to define what is covered by various costs, according to the areas mentioned before:

I.   **Staffing costs**

1.   Standard staffing costs
  a.   Basic salary by type of employee
  b.   Compulsory health insurance, employers contribution to private health insurance
  c.   Social insurance
  d.   Pension contributions
  e.   Christmas bonus, vacation bonus
  f.   Other (severance pay, assistance with removal expenses,overtime pay, expenses for persons acting on an honorary basis)
2.   Staffing costs from special funds.

II.   **Costs of materials: collection development and collection maintenance**

1.   Collection development costs for:
  - Research literature (monographs, continuations, series)
  - Periodicals, journals
  - Electronic publications and services (CD-ROM, videos, software, multimedia etc.)

- Microforms
- Other Non-Book-Materials (maps, sheet music, games etc.)

2. Collection maintenance costs for:
- Binding
- Cleaning
- Restoration
- Filming
- Deacidification.

III. Library automation costs

1. Hardware: costs of repair and maintenance
2. Software maintenance
3. Networking costs

IV. Operating costs/Building maintenance

1. Cleaning expenses (external, internal)
2. Water
- drinking water
- sewage
3. Heating costs
4. Power
5. Building maintenance and upkeep
6. Maintenance expenses: roads, parking areas, lawns
7. Waste disposal
8. Security
9. Buildings insurance
10. Fire, theft, liability, accident etc. insurance
11. Repair and maintenance of equipment
12. Rentals: copier, readerprinter, garages, room hire
13. Taxes
14. Other

V. Imputed depreciation allowance (Investment costs and construction costs are allocated here)

1. Building depreciation
2. Depreciation of technical equipment and devices
3. Depreciation of library-specific-equipment: shelves, microfiche-readers etc.
4. Depreciation of business machines and office equipment (including computer hardware)
5. Depreciation of service vehicles

Overhead, like management and administrative costs, can best be allocated proportionally to the different cost centres.

VI. Administrative costs

1. Telecommunications
2. Mail
3. Stationery, office supplies, sundry supplies, other
4. Travel expenses
5. Costs for service vehicles (fuel, oil, tyres, servicing, insurance, tax)
6. Public relations (meetings, publications, representation)
7. Training and staff development
8. Consultants and legal advice
9. Membership dues
10. Reimbursement of expenses
11. General and administrative overheads

Due to our focus on the user we restrict the extent of our analysis of cost-effectiveness to the services provided by an academic library. We leave the cost-effectiveness of other functions such as acquisitions or cataloguing aside. Having determined what costs are connected with the various areas of the library's staff and material goods, it is important to define the input from each of these areas into the major user services provided by the library. These services can be summarized as follows:

- Access to the library's reading room(s)
- Borrowing items from the library's collection(s)
- Interlibrary loan
- Information and reference
- Access to equipment
- Additional services such as training.

In the case of all these services, costs of staff will play an important role. In all of them costs of space, furniture and equipment come into consideration. In the case of circulation, costs in relation with the library's collection(s) are at stake. Interlibrary loan particularly involves networking-costs. Access to reading room(s) demands relative high space and furniture costs, but little staff, etc. The extent to which each of the areas of the library's staff and material goods are involved in the various services is, therefore, different and requires careful calculations. Such calculations, however, provide the management with useful data about the allocation of its resources; i.e., which services are handled with relatively high costs of staff and which are primarily dependent on equipment costs.

Particularly in small libraries it will be difficult to reach a precise distinction between the costs involved with the various services, be it only because a member of staff may be deployed in more than one of the library's services, such as circulation and reference. In such cases a more or less rough estimate of the time involved in the different services and the equivalent level of costs may suffice.

Measuring Cost-effetiveness: Once the allocations to the various services of the library have been determined, the management has at its disposal the necessary financial data for measuring cost-effectiveness. Data regarding the extent to which the services are used is also needed, because measuring cost-effectiness means, after all, that we relate the investments into the library to quantitative data about the use of the services, its users, and also the total community served by the library..

Bringing the financial data and the data about the use of the library in relation with one another means that one divides the total per annum costs involved in a service of the library by

- the amount of use of that service
- the amount of users profiting from these services
- the amount of the total population of the academic community served by the library.

- all of those over the same period as the financial year in which the costs are measured.

Measuring cost-effectiveness per use and per user will frequently result in different figures. Often service to one user means, for instance, more than one (book)title or more than one enquiry.

Measuring cost-effectiveness in terms of the total academic community served by the library is useful, since most libraries are funded in order to serve the full community of which they are part (in the case of a faculty or institute library, the community is restricted to that faculty or institute). The community should, however, not be counted according to persons or heads, but to so-called full-time equivalents (FTE's), so as to eliminate the problems involved with counting full-time and part-time appointments.

Comparing the costs of a certain service per user and per FTE might bring to light interesting differences in financial terms between the real and the potential use of the library. A rule of thumb says: the lower the costs per FTE the better the performance from a purely financial point of view. One should, however, constantly be aware that the figures resulting from such quantitative measurements have only a limited value in themselves. In fact they become useful only when related to comparable figures from another source. Many such comparisons are possible. We restrict ourselves to three options:

❶ Comparisons between the same services during different years or parts of years. A more or less permanent measuring of cost-effectiveness provides the library's management with useful policy tools, for example, when the figures point to significant changes in performance over the years.

❷ Comparisons with other services within a library. Such comparisons may show where cost-effectiveness is best served, but tell us little about the quality of the services and the level of satisfaction of the users.

❸ Comparisons with figures of other academic libraries. Such comparisons are valid only if the parameters of the libraries involved are basically the same.

Measuring Cost-effectiveness of Various Services: In fact, each of the services provided by an academic library can be measured in terms of cost-effectiveness. In the following list the term service is taken in its widest sense, beginning with the accessibility of the library and including such activities as training in how to use the library's facilities and collections. The list is limited to the main functions of the library and serves as an example for those who want to go into more detail. The list can be extended and subdivided according to the needs of the library's management.

For each of the services in the following table basically apply the three categories of quantitative data, mentioned above:

- Use
- Users
- Total community (in terms of the total amount of FTE's in the academic community served by thelibrary).

SERVICE	COST PER
access to the library's reading room(s)	• visit to the library • visitor to the library • FTE of primary user group
circulation of items from the library's collection(s)	• request for circulation • title circulated • active borrower • FTE of primary user group
interlibrary loan (ILL)	• title requested via ILL • title delivered • active borrower • FTE of primary user group
reference and information service of the library	• enquiry • enquirer • FTE of primary user group

SERVICE	COST PER
access to library equipment such as CD-ROM	• unit of time (minute or hour) • user • FTE of primary user group
additional services, such as user education - training in the use of the library's collection and facilities	• hour of training • participant • FTE of primary user group

While discussing cost-effectiveness in the academic library, we restricted ourselves to user services. However, as stated above, cost-effectiveness measurement can also be applied to separate functions of an academic library which contribute to its services, but where users are not immediately involved, such as acquisition and cataloguing, automation or preservation, personnel administration, and, last but not least, the library's management.

Comparing Cost-effectiveness to the Quality of Services: In the beginning of this chapter we said that a library might reach a high degree of quality and of user satisfaction in spite of using its resources in an ineffective way.

On the other hand, low costs per cost unit, e.g. per title circulated or per enquiry answered, might encompass or even produce bad quality and low satisfaction. A high number of enquiries answered per hour could mean incorrect answers, and low costs per use of the reading-room might be achieved by inadequate space and bad heating. Costs per library service should always be set in relation to the quality of performance of the same service. The library should not be content to know that is is producing services in a cost-effective way, but also that those services are chosen, designed and delivered in the way that offers the greatest benefit to the primary user group.

For example: "Cost per Enquiry Answered" should be set in relation to the performance indicator "Correct Answer Fill Rate" and perhaps also to "User Satisfation with Reference Staff".

In this way, the library will be able to escape the danger of being one-sided, of stressing service quality while neglecting needful economy, or of ignoring users' needs in the bliss of being thrifty. Knowledge of both the quality and the cost of library services is needed for management decisions in setting priorities and allocating resources.

List of Performance Indicators

General Library Use and Facilities

Collection Quality

Catalogue Quality

Availability of Documents in the Collection

Reference Service

Remote Use

User Satisfaction

Structure of the Indicators

Name

Every indicator has been designated with a special name. Preference has been given to short expressive names that are already well-known in literature.

Definition

The definition describes the data that are necessary for the indicator and their relation.

It also explains whether some terms are used in a certain sense for this indicator.

Aims

Explains what the indicator is meant to measure in relation to the library's goals.

Describes what sort of libraries, special activities, or collections would benefit most from using the indicator.

Explains under what circumstances benchmarking with other libraries might be possible.

Method

Describes the way of collecting the data and of calculating the results and points to difficulties and to circumstances that would affect the results.

If more than one method has been validated and proved effective, several methods are described.

Interpretation and possible solutions

Discusses what the results of using the indicator may point to, especially reasons for low effectiveness.

Names possible reactions to the results in order to achieve higher effectiveness.

Further Reading

Those items marked with an asterisk are considered to be of special importance.

The ISO standard as well as other handbooks and manuals mentioned in the first part of the selected bibliography are taken for granted and have in general not been listed separately here.

Performance

Indicators

1. Market Penetration

Definition: Market penetration is defined by the proportion of the library's potential users who actually use the library.

- As potential users should be regarded the library's primary user group, i.e. those people who are first and foremost entitled to use the library (e.g. students and academic staff of a university).

- Active users are members of the primary user group who either have made use of the services of the library or have borrowed a document within a certain period of time (e.g. term, academic or calendar year).

By subdividing the primary user group according to status (students; academic staff; undergraduates; etc.) or subject (law; history; medicine) the market penetration can be further specified.

By asking for individual services that have been used, more detailed information will be available about market penetration concerning the different activities of the library.

Aims: The indicator determines how far the library's services are accepted by those it considers to be its primary user group. This is especially important in places where there is more than one library, as for example in two-tier systems, where students and staff can either use departmental libraries or the central library.

The market penetration rate for subgroups such as part-time students, postgraduates, or medical students, and the differentiation in regard to the services used provides still more valuable information for the library management and might lead to useful improvements of a particular service.

Structural differences between library systems should be taken into account when comparing libraries.

Method: There are two methods for assessing market penetration that differ in effort and accuracy.

- ❶ In libraries where borrowing documents is the predominant form of use, the analysis can be based on active borrowers (i.e. persons that have borrowed at least one document within the last year).

- ❷ If other forms of use (e.g. in-house use) are relevant for the library, a user survey should be conducted although it is more time-consuming. This can be done in the following two ways:

- Telephone interviews with a random sample of the primary user group. Telephone interviews have a higher rate of response than questionnaires distributed by mail.
- Mail questionnaires to a random sample of the primary user group.

Collection of data:

Method 1: The data about size and composition of the primary user group can be provided by the statistics department of the institution. They will probaly know the exact number of teaching staff and students as well as their status and their subjects.

Almost every variety of library statistics includes the number of users who have borrowed at least one document within a certain period of time (e.g. academic or calendar year). Splitting up active users into subgroups will only be possible by using the records of the automated circulation system.

If possible, active borrowers not belonging to the primary user group should not be considered.

Method 2: The telephone interview and the mail questionnaire should provide the following information:

- The status of the potential users (undergraduate, post-graduate, academic staff)
- Optional: the subject or department/research centre.

The following questions should be included:

Have you used library services within the last year?

Yes ☐
No ☐

Optional: If yes, which of the following services have you used? (several answers are possible):

I borrowed material from the library. ☐
I returned material to the library. ☐
I used material inside the library. ☐
I used the catalogue(s). ☐
I used the reference service. ☐
I used online information services. ☐

I worked privately in the reading room. ☐
I contacted the library via network. ☐

Calculation:

Method 1: The number of active borrowers is divided by the overall number of members belonging to the primary user group. The result is then multiplied by 100.

Example: A central library with a total catchment population of 44,928 students and 4,267 members of academic staff had 27,506 total active borrowers in 1995. The market penetration for this library which is part of a library system with 200 departmental libraries amounted to 55,9%.

Method 2: To obtain the percentage of market penetration for the second method, the number of persons answering that they have used library services is divided by the total number of persons being asked. The result is then multiplied by 100.

Interpretation and possible solutions: The higher the market penetration the better. However, high market penetration is not necessarily to be equated with good performance. If there is but one library which offers the material needed by the primary user group, more people will use the library than would be the case, if this library had to compete with other libraries possessing similar collections.

If a low penetration rate cannot be explained by the existence of other competing libraries there are several possible solutions:

- Improve services that are most attractive to users (e.g. more opening hours, a better undergraduate collection)

- Improve public relations to let the users know about the services the library offers (e.g. information on CD-ROM products or special collections owned by the library)

The rates for subgroups of the primary user group are escpecially useful, since they allow conclusions to be drawn about why the library does not satisfy the needs of these groups. A very high percentage of non-users in the subject history as compared to a high percentage of users in the subject economics hints at a considerable difference as regards the quality of the collection in each field.

Long distances between departments and the central library may account for a low market penetration in the subjects concerned.

Further reading:

Abbott, Christine: Performance Measurement in Library and Information Services. - London. Aslib, 1994, pp. 21 - 22.

* Blagden, John: Some Thoughts on Use and Users.
In: IATUL Quarterly, 2 (1988), pp. 125 - 134.

Bloor, Ian: Performance Indicators and Decision Support Systems for Libraries: A Practical Application of "Keys to Success". - London: British Library: British Library, 1991. (British Library Research Papers, 93), pp. 23 - 27.

Die effektive Bibliothek: Endbericht des Projekts "Anwendung und Erprobung einer Marketingkonzeption für öffentliche Bibliotheken" / Deutsches Bibliotheksinstitut. - 2 vols. - Berlin: Dt. Bibliotheksinstitut, 1992. (DBI-Materialien ; 119); especially the examples of community analysis in vol II.

Revill, Don H.: Performance Measures for Academic Libraries.
In: Encyclopedia of Library and Information Science / Ed. by Allen Kent. - Vol. 45, Suppl. 10. - New York: Dekker, 1990, p. 303.

Revill, Don H.: Some Examples and Types of Performance Measures.
In: Do We Really Need Libraries: Proceedings of the First Joint Library Association Cranfield Institute of Technology Conference on Performance Assessment / Ed. by John Blagden. Cranfield: Cranfield Press, 1983, p. 59.

2. Opening Hours Compared to Demand

Definition: The indicator relates the actual number and distribution of opening hours to the number and distribution of opening hours as desired by the users.

Opening hours in general means the average number of hours a library is open to the public from Monday to Sunday.

Aims: There is always a discrepancy between the opening hours wished for by the users and the library's ability to live up to these expectations because of financial and staff restrictions. This is true, although networking allows libraries to provide some of their services for 24 hours a day. There is still a heavy demand for borrowing documents and in-house use of documents at all times of the week. Measuring this demand may help to decide if and when the library should stay open longer.

This indicator is useful to all libraries.

Method: Ask a random sample of 200-300 actual users when entering or leaving the library about their opinion of the opening hours as they are and as they should be. Timing of data collection is very important. It should be spread equally over the day and throughout the week to make sure that people usually coming to the library in the morning are not disproportionately represented in comparison to users prefering the evening or Saturdays.

The questions could also be added to a user satisfaction survey (see indicator no. 16 "User Satisfaction").

1. How would you rate your satisfaction with the opening hours of the library?

   very unsatisfactory   ☐

   unsatisfactory   ☐

   moderately satisfactory   ☐

   satisfactory   ☐

   very satisfactory   ☐

2. Please specify the times other than the present opening hours you would like the library to be accessible, by placing an "O" in the appropriate box. The present opening hours are already represented by an "X".

	Mon	Tue	Wed	Thu	Fri	Sat	Sun
0 - 6							
7 - 8							
8 - 9	X	X	X	X	X		
9 - 10	X	X	X	X	X	X	
10 - 11	X	X	X	X	X	X	
11 - 12	X	X	X	X	X	X	
12 - 13	X	X	X	X	X	X	
13 - 14	X	X	X	X	X		
14 - 15	X	X	X	X	X		
15 - 16	X	X	X	X	X		
16 - 17	X	X	X	X	X		
17 - 18	X	X	X	X	X		
18 - 19	X	X	X	X	X		
19 - 20	X	X	X	X	X		
20 - 21	X	X	X	X	X		
21 - 22							
22 - 23							
23 - 24							

The questionnaire can be simplified by summarizing the preferences for additional opening hours:

> 2. What other times outside the present opening hours would you like the library to be accessible?

> Sunday opening   ☐
> Later Saturday opening   ☐
> Later Weekday opening   ☐

Many libraries have different opening hours during semester or vacation. Branch libraries or departments such as loan department or manuscript department may also have opening hours that differ from those of the library as a whole. In these cases it would be best to ask separate samples of users:

- Users coming to the library during vacation time
- Users entering the branch library
- Users entering a particular department of the library.

Interpretation and possible solutions: The library should react, if a high percentage of users asks for extended hours or criticizes the distribution of the current opening hours over the day or the week. This may be difficult, especially if users demand extended opening hours on weekends. A possible solution might be to open the library without offering full service, so that non-professional part-timers could run the library on these occasions.

The library should, however, know where to draw the line between "reasonable" and "unreasonable" demand. In order to know what is "reasonable",

- It would be possible to have extended opening hours (e.g. on Sunday) as a trial (e.g. for a test period of 2 or 3 months).

- Opening hours could be compared with those of other libraries in similar situations (central campus or spread over town).

- Opening hours could be compared with those of other cultural institutions (e.g. museum) of the town during the times in question.

This indicator does not show whether actual opening hours are too liberal and the supply exceeds the demand. That can be best assessed by closely observing attendance. In case the library can only offer further opening hours (e.g. weekend opening) in exchange for opening hours on other days, users could be asked what hours they would be willing to sacrifice in exchange for hours they prefer.

Further reading:

Åslund, Henrik: Öppettider/Service: Rapport från biblioteksundersökningen vid Stockholms universitetsbibliotek den 14-20 november 1994. - Stockholm: Universitetsbibliotek, 1994.

Bloor, Ian: Performance Indicators and Decision Support Systems for Libraries: A Practical Application of "Keys to Success". - London: British Library, 1991. (British Library Research Papers, 93), pp. 31 - 33.

Revill, Don H.: Some Examples and Types of Performance Measures.
In: Do We Really Need Libraries: Proceedings of the First Joint Library Association Cranfield Institute of Technology Conference on Performance Assessment / Ed. by John Blagden. - Cranfield: Cranfield Press, 1983, pp. 61 - 62.

3. Expert Checklists

Definition: This indicator does not assess the quality of the collection by analysing in how far it meets the actual demand of the users. Instead, a list drawn up by experts or from a generally acknowledged bibliography is applied as quality standard for the library's collection.

Collection quality is here defined as the percentage of titles enumerated in an expert list or in a bibliography which are in the possession of the library.

Aims: This indicator aims at finding out to what extent the collection of the library lives up to commonly accepted standards. Although it says nothing about the users' acceptance of the collection, this indicator can reveal deficiencies of collection development policies. It helps to revise collection development, so that the acquisition budget is spent effectively.

The advantages of this evaluation approach are:

- It provides a direct qualitative assessment of collection strength.
- It can be realised without much effort.
- It yields results which can easily be compared with those of other institutions, provided the collections are similar.

The main problems are:

- Expert lists as well as bibliographies are subjective.
- They can differ widely from the actual demand of the library users.
- Although checklists are particularly useful when measuring the quality of the collection in a small and highly specified subject area, this method is not suited to evaluate the quality of the total collection. The information that a library possesses 35.3% of all the titles in the national bibliography is less useful than the statement that 74% of the titles listed in 4 bibliographies on English language and literature are to be found in the collection.

Method: The choice of the expert list or the bibliography which is to serve as standard is of crucial importance for the reliability of the evaluation process:

- The degree of specialization as well as the languages used should be determined according to the nature of the collection and the acquisition policy of the library. Mission,goals and objectives of a library should be taken into consideration.
- The subject should be clearly defined.

- The titles in the list should not date before the time the library started its collection in the particular subject.
- The list should not contain more than 500 to 1,000 titles.

The interests of the institution are largely represented, if course reading lists of university departments or lists prepared by academic staff in the university for their particular subject areas are used as expert list.

Each title of the list is looked up in the catalogue. This should be done by professional librarians whose skills in using the catalogue will guarantee that all titles actually recorded in the catalogue will be found.

Calculation: The number of titles in the list or bibliography which are in the collection is divided by the total number of titles in the list or bibliography. The result multiplied by 100 is the title fill rate.

Interpretation and possible solutions: A high title fill rate is desirable. If collection and expert list only match to a small degree, the titles in the list or bibliography may not be relevant for the library in question. But if they are relevant, reasons must be found why the subject has been neglected. Provided that the necessary funds are available, there is one simple solution to make up for the mistakes of the past; namely to buy those books from the list which are not in your collection. However, that should not be done thoughtlessly. Before spending a lot of money on books which you do not know will be used, you should check the actual demand. In this context the performance indicator "Subject Collection Use" should be used. The reliability of the results might also be checked by a comparison with another library which is similar to one's own in regard to size, collection profile, etc.

Further reading:

* **Bonn, George S.:** Evaluation of the Collection.
In: Library Trends, 22 (1973), pp. 265 - 304.

Comer, Cynthia: List Checking as a Method for Evaluating Library Collections.
In: Collection Building, 3 (1981), pp. 26-34.

* **Lancaster, F. Wilfrid; Sharon L. Baker:** The Measurement and Evaluation of Library Services. - 2nd ed. - Arlington, Vrg.: Information Resources Press, 1991, pp. 42 - 47.

Goldhor, Herbert: Analysis of an Inductive Method of Evaluating the Book Collection of a Public Library.
In: Libri, 23 (1973), pp. 6 - 17.

Tjarks, Larry: Evaluating Literature Collections.
In: RQ, 12 (1972), pp. 183 - 185.

Wiemers, Eugene Jr.; Carol Ann Baldwin; Barbara Kautz; Linda Haack Lomker: Collection Evaluation: A Practical Guide to the Literature. In: Library Acquisitions, 8 (1984), pp. 65 - 76.

4. Collection Use

Definition: Collection use is defined as the ratio between the number of document uses within a certain period of time and the total number of documents in the collection.
Document use in the sense of this indicator consists of circulation and in-house use.

Aims: This indicator determines the degree of use of the collection and, therefore, the quality of the collection. In contrast to using expert lists or bibliographies (see indicator no. 3 "Expert Checklists"), collection quality is here defined in terms of the actual demand made by the users.

This indicator will be most useful for collections of current research literature. For those parts of a collection where the development policy is determined by an archival function, actual demand will not be the most important criterion for evaluating collection quality.

The indicator is meant to assess all cases of collection use, not only loans. It is also extremely important for academic libraries to know the amount of in-house use. These data have long been neglected, because they are not easily retrieved. Even in libraries with closed stacks, in-house use of the reading-room material may represent a considerable factor. In open-access libraries with liberal study facilities, in-house use can easily reach the same level as circulation, and in collections where journals are predominant, browsing, reading, and copying in the library will be the most important form of use.

Only if loans and in-house uses combined are compared with the stock will the library know to what extent its collection is used.

Method: For this indicator, the following datasets have to be collected:

- The number of loans within a certain period of time (usually a year)
- The number of in-house uses within the same period
- The total number of documents in the collection.

Collection of data: Two of these datasets will be easily obtained. In their annual statistics most libraries count the total number of documents in the collection. Depending on whether circulation is managed by hand or by an automated circulation system, libraries will count the annual number of loans. For this indicator circulation includes renewals and interlibrary loans, but excludes, if possible, documents charged out to internal library units (e.g. binding or cataloguing department).

The main problem is to ascertain in-house use. In regard to this indicator, in-house use means every use of a document inside the library, including short browsing at the shelves or photo-copying by users. Documents that have been recorded in the circulation system, but are used in the library, are counted as loans, as it would not be possible to separate them from other loans.

Several methods have been suggested to count in-house use:

❶ Self-reporting by users

When leaving the library, users are asked how many documents they used during their visit.
The method is time-consuming, and the results will probably be inaccurate, as users will not remember everything they did during their visit.

❷ Marking on slips or labels

A slip is inserted in the book, or a label is affixed to the front cover. The users are then asked to put a mark on the slip or label every time they have used the book.
The method is time-consuming and could best be used in specific parts of the collection, e.g. current issues of periodicals. The data retrieved will probably show lower use than in reality, as users could forget to put marks on the slips or labels.

❸ Unobtrusive observation

Members of staff are assigned specified parts of the open stacks or reading rooms in order to count in-house use. They must be well instructed in order to avoid differences in counting.
The method is extremely time-consuming and therefore not suitable for long-term studies or regular measuring. If the observation is noticed, users' behaviour might be influenced. The advantage of this method is that casual browsing can be fully included though what is counted as a use might be defined differently by the observers.

❹ Reshelving by staff

Users are asked not to reshelve books or other documents, but to leave them on the tables in the reading rooms or the open stacks. The number of books left on the tables is counted by staff at certain intervals.
This method is less time-consuming than the others and therefore suitable for regular measuring. There are some defects, though:

- Casual browsing at the shelves is not fully included, as users are apt to reshelve the books.

- Most libraries with open access collections try to induce their users to reshelve the books. Regular sampling of in-house use might make the users forget this habit.

- Heavily used documents could be used by several users before being reshelved. Staff would have to reshelve quickly in order to avoid this.

In spite of some shortcomings, reshelving by staff seems to be the most practical and reliable method. If data cannot be collected in regular intervals over the year, there should be at least two representative weeks for a sample.

In some library systems it would be possible to read the barcodes of all documents before reshelving. The system could then produce counts of in-library use for different subject areas, provided the information on the subject of the titles in question is available. This method is time-consuming, and will perhaps only be used in cases of special interests.

For measuring in-house use of current issues of periodicals, method 2 (slips or labels) has also proved reliable and practical. It can also be used for assessing the amount of use of specific journals.

Calculation: In-house use will probably be counted by sampling. If users' habits vary much over the year, it might be inaccurate to extrapolate the data of the sample to achieve the annual total.

Most studies of in-house use have assumed a correlation between circulation and in-house use. Though this correlation could change over time, owing to altered circumstances in the library or users' studying habits, it could be used to check the number of in-house uses gained by sampling.

The number of in-house uses during the sampling period is put in relation to the number of loans during the same period. The ratio of in-house use to circulation thus calculated can be used to deduce the number of annual in-house uses from the annual circulation.

The number of in-house uses per year added to the number of loans per year is the total number of collection uses. To calculate the ratio of collection use to the size of collection, the total number of collection uses is divided by the number of documents in the collection.

Example: The automated system of a library has recorded 400,000 loans during the last 12 months. According to two sample periods the in-house use in these months amounted to 160,000. The collection use of the library is 560,000. Divided by the 420,000 documents in the possession of the library, its degree of collection use amounts to 1.3. This library achieves a better result than another library with 230,000 loans and 70,000 instances of in-house use whose collection consists of 290,000 documents and whose degree of collection use, therefore, is only 1.0.
The higher the figure is, the better the extent of utilization.

Interpretation and possible solutions: For various reasons the collection may seem to be used insufficiently:

- The stock is not adapted to users' needs.
- The stock is outdated.
- There are not enough copies of titles that are much in demand.
- The loan periods are too long.
- Other libraries have taken over the library's functions for certain subjects or tasks, so that, though the collection is of good quality, it is less used.

The amount of collection use deemed as sufficient, depends on the library's mission and goals. Archival functions prevent a library from weeding. Functions in special collection plans or legal deposit rights force the library to collect material that is seldom used. In subject areas such as history or philosophy, titles remain interesting for a longer period of time. Therefore, decisions regarding weeding should not be based on low collection use within the first years.

If collection use is insufficient, information about the causes can be gained by using this indicator for special subjects or parts of the collections, e.g.:

- Current periodicals
- Undergraduate library
- Biological literature.

This would demand that the circulation system yield data about these parts of the collection, and that in-house use can be counted separately.

Causes for insufficient collection use can also be found by using other performance indicators:

- Expert Checklists (shows whether the collection meets certain standards)
- Availability (shows whether the users get the material they ask for)
- Percentage of Collection Not Used (shows whether parts of the collection are not used at all).

Higher collection use can scarcely be achieved without spending money, unless the library decides to discard the unused books, thus attaining a relatively increased usage. Otherwise,

- the collection must be improved by replacing old issues and buying new material.

- the stock must be adapted to the needs of the primary user group.

The last task in particular is rather difficult and can only be solved in close cooperation with the institution. The library's acquisition profile should be influenced by the curricula. Each lecturer could send a copy of the reading lists for his/her courses to the subject specialist who will check them against the present collection and buy those books not yet in the collection.

Interlibrary lending requests and users' proposals for acquisitions should, of course, be evaluated daily.

If the indicator is used regularly, it will be of interest for the library to observe alterations in the ratio of circulation to in-house use. This ratio can be influenced by many factors:

- Study habits of the users (preference for home or in the library)
- Equipment and user seats in the library
- Opening hours of the library
- Percentage of the collection with open access for users
- Percentage of the collection reserved for in-house use.

Further reading:

Broadus, Robert N.: Use Studies of Library Collections.
In: Library Resources and Technical Services, 24 (1980), pp. 317 - 324.

Fussler, Herman H; Julian L. Simon: Patterns in the Use of Books in Large Research Libraries. - Chicago: The University of Chicago Press, 1969.

* Garg, K.C.: Quantitative Methods in Information Science: An Overview.
In: Collection Management, 14 (1991), pp. 75 - 100.

Hindle, Anthony; Michael K. Buckland: In-Library Book Usage in Relation to Circulation.
In: Collection Management, 2 (1978), pp. 265 - 277.

Kent, Allen et. al.: Use of Library Materials: the University of Pittsburgh Study. - New York: Dekker, 1979.

Lancaster, F. Wilfrid: If You Want to Evaluate Your Library ... - 2nd. edition. - Champaign, Il.: University of Illinois, 1993, esp. pp. 76 - 85.

Lane, Lorraine L.: The Relationship Between Loans and In-house Use of Books in Determining a Use-factor for Budget Allocation.
In: Library Acquisitions : Practice and Theory, 11 (1987), pp. 95-102.

Selth, Jeff; Nancy Koller, Peter Briscoe: The Use of Books Within the Library.
In: College and Research Libraries, 53 (1992), pp. 197 - 205.

Tjoumas, Renee; Esther E. Horne: Collection Evaluation: Practices and Methods in Libraries of ALA Accredited Graduate Library Education Programs
In: Advances in Library Administration and Organization, 5 (1986), pp. 109 - 138

Wortman, William A.: Collection Management: Background and Principles. - Chicago, London: American Library Association, 1989, esp. pp. 109 - 114.

5. Subject Collection Use

Definition: A subject area's degree of use is the relation between the subject's proportion of the circulation, its proportion of the annual intake, and the proportion of the annual budget spent on the subject.

Depending on the relation of these factors a subject area can be overused or underused. For a subject area to be overused there must be a disproportion between the demand for a subject area, measured in terms of loans within a certain period of time, and the supply, expressed in terms of money spent on documents for the subject area and in terms of items added to the subject collection in question. If the supply exceeds the demand, the subject area is underused.

In the context of this indicator, circulation represents use, independent of other forms such as in-house use. The indicator is therefore particularly useful for the evaluation of monograph collections, since periodicals are in most cases used inside the library.

Aims: This indicator determines whether a library's resource allocation and acquisition policy meet the demand of the users. The library finds out if it spends the money on the right monographs and the right subject areas.

The indicator is applicable to all libraries, provided borrowing, at least of monographs, is the predominant form of use. Comparisons between libraries are only feasible if their collection profile and acquisition policy are similar and the subjects covered are comparable.

According to its definition the indicator makes sense only for collections of current research literature. Only libraries that are kept up-to-date by constant weeding and do not contain any special collections should measure the use of the whole collection, split up into subjects. The best method for large libraries is to take a random sample of recently acquired research literature and to relate the use for each subject area to the book funds spent on the subject area and the annual intake for that subject area. *The second method is described as follows:*.

Method: This indicator concentrates on the monographs in the lending collection that the library has bought for current demand. The sample should therefore exclude, as far as possible:

- Journals
- Monographs which are older than three or, at most, five years
- Documents reserved for in-house use
- Special collections, which have been built up because of special tasks attributed to the library (legal deposit, special collection programmes, etc.), and which are not intended to be used by the primary user group in the first place
- Acquisitions by gift or exchange.

If possible, it is useful to leave out the undergraduate collection, because in the case of some subject areas it will have considerable influence on the number of loans.

The sample shall cover acquisitions of a certain period (e.g. one year). The number of uses for the monographs in the sample shall be gathered from two years following the year of acquisition. Thus, we can be sure that the acquired monographs are registered in the catalogues and are covered by bibliographies and reviews. It seems reasonable to concentrate on the usage within the first two years after a title has been acquired, because the chance that a monograph which has not been borrowed within the first two years will ever be borrowed is usually one to four.

The number of monographs acquired per year is the criterion to determine the sample size. In order to receive reliable results, 10% of the annual intake of monographs should be analysed.

If different circumstances, for instance no computer system, make it more difficult to gather the necessary data, the sample size can be smaller.

A random sample is taken from the lending collection. If the library in question is shelving by order of accession, it is quite easy to find the desired number of shelf marks which belong to monographs acquired within a certain period. In the case of a classified shelving system where the title data as well as the acquisition data are provided by the computer system, this problem is also solved easily. If the data in question are only to be found in the accession books, the task is somewhat more difficult and time-consuming.

Collection of data: For every monograph the number of loans is counted within the period of two years. The data are obtained from the records of the automated circulation system or from date stamps in the books. Where only the number of loans per shelf mark is known, it must be divided by the number of copies and the number of volumes belonging to that shelf mark. In order to evaluate the intensity of book use, the results should be summarized. The following graduation seems reasonable: 1-5, 6-10, 11-15, 16-30 loans.

Titles never borrowed should be examined more closely. Is the title actually in the catalogue? Is the book in its place?

Calculation: Relation between book use and subject area

Each title must be assigned to a subject area or group of subject areas. We want to find the percentage (L) of each subject area in the total number of loans:

$$L = \frac{\text{number of loans in one subject area}}{\text{total number of loans within the sample}}$$

If, for example, 131 loans of the total of 1,393 loans can be assigned to the field of religion and theology the percentage (L) of this subject would be 9.4041 or rounded off to 9.40%.

Relation between book use for each subject area and acquisition funds spent on the subject area as well as annual intake for the subject area

The number of loans for each subject area is related to the amount of money spent on monographs for this subject area. In order to avoid variations one should take the average expenditure of several years (preferably three and more). The same has to be done for the annual intake in volumes per subject area. It is preferable to take into account not only the funds but also the intake, since there are considerable price differences for the different subject areas. For instance, books on psychology are on the average much cheaper than books on chemistry. The following table lists possible results for the subjects of philosophy (classification no. 2), economics (7), law (8), computer science (13), art (28), English language and literature (32), and history (39):

no. of subject	percent of acquisition funds	percent of intake (volumes)	percent of loans
2	3.50	3.20	3.37
7	6.95	7.55	17.01
8	8.15	4.90	3.58
13	1.55	1.65	3.94
28	3.05	2.35	1.29
32	1.80	1.75	2.15
39	11.70	9.15	13.20

To make an evaluation easier, the three values are put in relation to each other. The percentage of loans (L) is divided by the percentage of annual intake (I) as well as by the percentage of the annual budget spent on acquisitions (A) for a subject. The mean of the two values resulting from this division is the degree of use (DU):

subject	L/A	L/I	DU
2	0.96	1.05	1.00
7	2.44	2.25	2.34
8	0.43	0.73	0.58
13	2.54	2.38	2.46
28	0.42	0.54	0.48
32	1.19	1.22	1.20
39	1.12	1.44	1.28

The higher the value for the degree of use the better the relation between intake, expenditure and use for the subject area in question. Thus the degree of use in the case of law (8) is four times worse than in the case of economics (7).

One can speak of a subject area's "balanced" degree of use, if the percentage of loans, intake and expenditure for this subject area or group of subject areas is the same. In that case the degree of use equals 1. Therefore, every subject area or group of subject areas with a degree of use below 1 is considered **underused**, with a degree of use above 1 it is **overused**. In our example, subject area 2 has a balanced degree of use, subjects 7, 13, 32 and 39 are overused and 8 and 28 are underused.

Interpretation and possible solutions: The acquisition profile possibly has to be changed, if a subject area is underused. Either the collection does not contain the titles asked for by the users, or users of this subject area do not come into the library.

- An examination of the zero-loans might lead to the conclusion that the users scorn books written in certain languages, or dealing with very specialized subject matters, or having too many pages.

- The collection might contain current literature in certain fields of research which are not represented in the curriculum of the institution.

Great differences in the degree of use between certain subject areas suggest making changes in resource allocation. It does not make sense if a large amount of money is spent on a heavily underused subject area, while highly overused subject areas lack money. Several factors are affecting the indicator, which ask a repeated application before revising allocation systems:

- Restriction to circulation, leaving out in-house use
- Restriction to lending collection
- Problem of defining subject areas
- Intricacies of sampling
- Too vague acquisition profiles.

Use is but one criterion for the decision whether a title should be in the collection or not, but it should not be underestimated.

Further reading:

* **Aguilar, William:** The Application of Relative Use and Interlibrary Demand in Collection Development.
In: Collection Management, 8 (1986), pp. 15 - 24.

* **Bonn, George S.:** Evaluation of the Collection.
In: Library Trends, 22 (1974), pp. 265 - 304.

Burr, Robert L.: Evaluating Library Collections: A Case Study.
In: The Journal of Academic Librarianship, 5 (1979), pp. 256 - 260.

*Day, Mike; Don Revill: Towards the Active Collection: The Use of Circulation Analyses in Collection Evaluation.
In: Journal of Librarianship and Information Science. - 27 (1995), pp. 149 - 157.

Fussler, Herman H and Julian L. Simon: Patterns in the Use of Books in Large Research Libraries. - Chicago: University of Chicago Press, 1969.

* Galvin, Thomas J. and Allen Kent: Use of a University Library Collection.
In: Library Journal, 102 (1977), pp. 2317 - 2320.

Jain, A. K.: Sampling and Data Collection Methods for a Book-Use Study.
In: The Library Quarterly, 39 (1969), pp. 245 - 252.

* Lancaster, F. Wilfrid; Sharon L. Baker: The Measurement and Evaluation of Library Services. - 2nd ed. - Arlington, Vrg.: Information Resources Press, 1991, esp. pp. 79 - 121.

Nimmer, Ronald J.: Circulation and Collection Patterns at the Ohio State University Libraries.
In: Library Acquisitions: Practice and Theory, 4 (1980), pp. 61 - 70.

Trueswell, Richard W.: Determining the Optimal Number of Volumes for a Library's Core Collection.
In: Libri, 16 (1966) p. 49 - 60.

Wenger, Charles B.; Christine B. Sweet and Helen J. Stiles: Monograph Evaluation for Acquisitions in a Large Library.
In: Journal of the American Society for Information Science, 30 (1979), pp. 88 - 92.

6. Documents Not Used

Definition: This indicator is the percentage of documents in the lending collection not issued within a certain period of time.

Aims: This indicator determines which part of the lending collection has not been used in the sense of not being borrowed. It is restricted to circulation of the lending collection, since it would be almost impossible to record in-house use of single documents over a long period of time.

The indicator complements indicator no. 4 "Collection Use". "Collection Use" compares the number of documents in the collection with the number of uses, irrespective of the fact that some documents have been used often while others have not been used at all. In contrast this indicator refers to the single document and its use, as there may be "dead areas" in the collection though the collection as a whole is heavily used. This indicator will be able to support weeding decisions as well as changes in resource allocation.

The indicator is based on the assumption that a library's performance is better if a higher percentage of the collection has been issued. This, of course, is only true when the primary goal of collection building and maintenaince is current use. If the library has archival functions, or if there is a considerable collection of rare books, this indicator should be applied only to the part of the collection that is meant for current use by members of the primary user group, e.g.:

- Undergraduate collection
- Current research literature acquired within the last ten years.

Any documents that came into the library as legal deposit should be left out, since the question of their use is irrelevant.

If the size of the subject collections is known, the indicator can be split up into different subjects.

Each library should be aware of the parts of the collection that are not used at all. A comparison between libraries is only possible if the collections under consideration are similar in kind, size and structure.

Method: For this indicator, the following datasets have to be collected:

- The number of documents in the lending collection
- The number of documents in the lending collection not issued within a certain period of time (one year to five years).

Collection of data: The size of the lending collection will probably be known. Documents restricted to in-house use (e.g. collections of rare books) should be excluded from the total collection of the library.

In order to find out the documents that have not been issued within the given period of time, the library has to rely on data from an automated library system. For a relatively small collection it might be possible to assess document use manually if each issue has been recorded in the document by stamp or other marks.

Sampling should only be used with caution, as there may exist clusters of unused documents in different parts of the collection.

The period under surveillance will depend on the collection in question. It should be short (e.g. one year) for an undergraduate library and longer (e.g. five years) for a collection in subjects such as archaeology.

Calculation: The number of unissued documents in the lending collection is divided by the number of documents in this collection. The result is then multiplied by 100.

Example: 3,149 documents out of 74,114 documents within the lending collection have not been borrowed within the last three years. Multiplied by 100, the percentage of documents not used amounts to 4.25.

Interpretation and possible solutions: If a high percentage of documents has not been issued, the library ought first to find out whether high in-house use has reduced circulation. The next step will be to assess what kind of documents have not be issued, for instance:

- Documents that have been acquired for special (archival) functions
- Older documents that have become obsolete
- Documents in certain subject collections.

It should also be taken into account whether parts of the collection are housed in parts of the building that are less accessible, or whether documents registered only in card catalogues have been used less than those registered in online catalogues.

To assess particular reasons for non-use, it would, of course, be best to apply the indicator to different subjects and to compare the proportion of unissued documents for these subjects. This is possible if the automated library system provides data according to subject.

Management decisions resulting from a high percentage of non-use could be:

- To weed obsolete documents

- To adapt the acquisition policy to the needs of the primary user group
- To shift resources from subjects with a high proportion of unissued documents to highly used subjects
- To promote the use of those parts of the collection that seem to be unknown to users because of their locality or catalogue situation.

Further reading: The indicator has not been described in this form in the existing literature. But calculations of non-use have, of course, appeared in articles and books on performance measurement, often with models of predicting future use.

The indicator as described above resulted from the investigations of the indicators "Collection Use" and "Subject Collection Use" for these guidelines.

Broadus, Robert N.: Use Studies of Library Collections.
In: Library Resources and Technical Services, 24 (1980), pp. 317 - 324.

Fussler, Herman H; Julian L. Simon: Patterns in the Use of Books in Large Research Libraries. - Chicago: The University of Chicago Press, 1969.

Kent, Allen et. al.: Use of Library Materials: the University of Pittsburgh Study. - New York: Dekker, 1979, especially pp. 9 - 24.

Trueswell, Richard W.: A Quantitative Measure of User Circulation Requirements and Its Possible Effect on Stack Thinning and Multiple Copy Determination.
In: American Documentation, 16 (1965), pp. 20 - 25.

7. Known-Item-Search

Definition: The proportion of titles sought by the user and registered in the catalogue that the user manages to find is called the success rate of known-item-searches.

This success rate depends on two factors:

- The user's skill in handling the catalogue
- The quality of the catalogue.

Aims: This indicator determines the library's success in making the catalogue an effective finding tool and informing the users how to find a title.

An analysis of the user's skill in handling the catalogue provides information about the accuracy of the bibliographic details the search is based on, the knowledge of different kinds of catalogues, the knowledge of cataloguing rules. Especially the problems of specific user groups like undergraduates or part-time students with the catalogue will become evident. Consequently, the indicator helps to decide where user education has to be improved.

The indicator also helps to find out whether

- the catalogue is complete
- the catalogue is defective (e.g. missing cross references prevent the users from finding the titles they are looking for)
- an online catalogue in terms of interface (commands, help screens etc.) presents the bibliographic information in a user-friendly way.

Libraries with closed stacks will benefit more from applying the indicator than libraries with free access to the whole collection, because there the catalogue always stands between the user and the material he or she is looking for. A comparison between libraries requires careful consideration of any differences between cataloguing rules or types of catalogues.

This indicator can be split up into specific user groups like undergraduates, part-time students, or members of the academic staff.

Method: The procedure is similar to that of an availability study (see indicator no. 11). Users approaching the catalogue or OPAC-terminal are asked if they are looking for a specific monograph or journal. They are given a form on which to write

- their status (undergraduate, postgraduate, staff)
- the bibliographic details they have
- if they have found the document (shelf mark) or not.

They are asked to return the forms when leaving the library.

Information about 200 titles seems sufficient to obtain reliable results. It is important that the data should not be collected at the beginning of the academic year or term when there are a lot of new users who are not yet familiar with the search procedures.

As in an availability study, successes and failures are counted. Those titles that could not be found are checked by an experienced cataloguer who assesses whether the title is actually registered in the catalogue and whether the failure was due to a mistake by the user (wrong or insufficient bibliographic data, insufficient knowledge of cataloguing rules, disregard of cross references, etc.) or by the library (missing cross references, wrong catalogue entries, etc.)

Calculation:

Success rate: The number of titles that were found in the catalogue divided by the total number of titles in the sample. The result is multiplied by 100.

User failure rate: The number of titles not found because of user mistakes divided by the total number of titles in the sample. The result is multiplied by 100.

Library failure rate: The number of titles not found because of library mistakes divided by the total number of titles in the sample. The result is multiplied by 100.

Interpretation and possible solutions: The alphabetical catalogue (author/title) is a basic means of stock exploitation. Any document which the library has acquired, but for one reason or another does not turn up in the catalogue, is lost unless it is found by chance on the shelf.

Possible reasons for a low success rate may be wrong or incomplete catalogue entries, missing cross references or illegible catalogue cards. The reaction should be to improve the quality of the catalogue, e.g. by regularly checking a sample of entries.

Furthermore, the library is partly responsible for a high user failure rate. Too complicated search procedures in an OPAC or lacking support by help screens lower the success rate. So does an intricate catalogue situation in a stage of transition between card or microfiche catalogue and OPAC.

The library is not to blame if titles are not found because of fragmentary bibliographical data, for which not even an OPAC will produce the desired result.

There are several solutions for improving the success rate. The best way would be, of course, to use simple cataloguing rules the user can easily understand. The current cataloguing rules, which are based on national and international standards are complicated but cannot be changed fundamentally. Libraries must therefore concentrate on user education and help functions:

- Better labelling of catalogues (if there are several catalogues)
- Better help screens in OPACs
- Continuous user education to enhance knowledge of different catalogue types and their rules.

Further Reading:

Chacha, Rosemary N.; Ann Irving: An Experiment in Academic Library Performance Measurement.
In: British Journal of Academic Librarianship, 6 (1991), pp. 13 - 26.

* **Lancaster, F. Wilfrid; Sharon L. Baker:** The Measurement and Evaluation of Library Services. - 2nd ed. - Arlington, Vrg.: Information Resources Press, 1991, pp. 181 - 206.

Lipetz, Ben-Ami: Catalog Use in a Large Research Library.
In: Library Quarterly, 42 (1972), pp. 129 - 139.

Seymour, Carol A.; J.L. Schofield: Measuring Reader Failure at the Catalogue.
In: Library Resources and Technical Services, 17 (1973), pp. 6 - 24.

Wildemuth, Barbara M.; Ann L. O'Neill: The "Known" in Known-Item Searches: Empirical Support for User-Centred Design.
In: College and Research Libraries, 56 (1995), pp. 265 - 281.

8. Subject Search

Definition: This indicator determines the proportion of titles in the subject or classified catalogue matching the user's subject that are found by the user.

Aims: The purpose of the indicator is to assess the quality of the catalogue and of user information by the proportion of successful searches. A subject search in catalogues is deemed successful when two criteria are fulfilled:

- It must have a high degree of recall, i.e., as many titles as possible of all the titles in the catalogue which deal with this subject must be found.

- It must have a high degree of precision, i.e., as many titles found in the catalogue as possible must deal precisely with the subject in question.

Measuring the success rate of subject searches helps to find weaknesses of the system the subject catalogue is based on, of the retrieval method, of the way the user is guided through the system, and of the user's knowledge of the rules underlying the catalogue.

The indicator is of use to all libraries with subject or classified catalogues, especially to libraries with closed stacks, where the users cannot look on the shelves for literature relevant to their theme but are forced to use the catalogue. The indicator can be used irrespective of the type of catalogue (card catalogue, microfiche catalogue, or online catalogue).

A comparison between libraries requires careful consideration of any differences between cataloguing rules or types of catalogues.

The indicator can be split up into specific user groups like undergraduates, part-time students, or members of a faculty.

Method: The evaluation of searches in classified or subject catalogues is a time-consuming task. The ultimate success of a search is difficult to determine, since sometimes not even the experienced librarian will be capable of retrieving all the information on a particular topic.

Methods like unobtrusive observation, transaction log analysis, and asking the user to talk aloud and analysing the protocol of the recorded search have all been used, especially to obtain information about the search process.

In order to assess the success rate, the following method has been found sufficiently valid and yet manageable:

❶ A questionnaire is handed out to a random sample of users after the search asking for

- a short description of the subject they were seeking for
- the subject headings or notations they consulted
- the subject headings or notations under which they found the titles they thought relevant
- the number of relevant titles found.

❷ A short interview with a professional librarian, preferably a subject specialist, is then added in order to define the user's subject clearly.

❸ The librarian reconstructs the search in order to check whether all subject headings or notations that match the subject have been consulted.

As the measuring process is time-consuming, a sample of 100 to 200 persons should be sufficient.

The librarian's decision whether a title matches the user's subject is certainly not objective and biased by the librarian's knowledge of the topic. Yet, as the precise number of references in the catalogue matching the user's subject is not known, the titles the librarian considers relevant can be used as an estimate.

Collection of data:

Two data must be collected:

❶ Number of titles found by the user:

All titles grouped under subject headings or notations that the user found relevant, and that the librarian confirmed to be relevant, are counted as found, even if the user did not borrow all the documents.

❷ Number of titles indexed in the catalogue matching the user's subject:

The titles additionally found by the librarian under other subject headings or notations are added to the titles found by the user.

Calculation: The number of titles found by the user is divided by the number of titles indexed in the catalogue matching the user's subject. The result is multiplied by 100.

Interpretation and possible solutions: There are a number of reasons why the success rate of subject searches might not be acceptable, some of which are outside the range of the library's influence:

The user
- General intelligence and perseverance
- Insufficient information about the catalogues
- Wrong choice of search terms (too narrow, too broad, wrong spelling; unfamiliar or newly coined words)
- Disregard of cross references.

The classification or indexing system
- Complicated rules
- Vocabulary obsolete or system out-of-date
- Vocabulary or system not adequate to the user group
- Subject headings not specific enough
- Lack of cross references
- Misleading cross references.

The catalogue system
- Several catalogues with differing cataloguing rules
- Unsophisticated retrieval software
- Unsatisfactory user interface.

Special activities of the library to enhance the success rate would primarily be directed at user information and education. Tutorials for new students should include how to do subject searches not only in library catalogues, but also in bibliographies and databases.

The library will probably not be free to choose other rules for subject cataloguing, but improving cross references or adding subject entries might be possible. Clear self-explanatory labelling and help screens would be another means for improving the success rate.

Further reading:

Aanonson, John: A Comparison of Keyword Subject Searching on Six British University Opacs. In: Online Review, 11 (1987), pp. 303 - 313.

Bosman, F.E.; Ongering, M.A.H.; Smit, H.P.A.: Observeren en registreren: Evaluatieonderzoek naar OPC3. In: Open, 25 (1993), pp. 352 - 356.

Hancock-Beaulieu, Micheline: Evaluation of Online Catalogues: An Assessment of Methods / Micheline Hancock-Beaulieu; Stephen Robertson; Colin Neilson. - London: British Library, 1990. (British Library Research Paper ; 78), esp. pp. 5 - 64.

Lewis, David W.: Research on the Use of Online Catalogs and Its Implications for Library Practice.
In: Journal of Academic Librarianship, 13 (1987), 152 - 157.

Markey, Karen: Subject Searching in Library Catalogs. - Dublin, Ohio: Online Computer Library Center, 1984.

Markey, Karen: The Process of Subject Searching in the Library Catalog: Final Report of the Subject Access Research Project. - Dublin, Ohio: Online Computer Library Center, 1983, esp. pp. 16 - 24.

Moore, Carol Weiss: User Reactions to Online Catalogs: An Exploratory Study.
In: College and Research Libraries, 42 (1981), pp. 295 - 302.

Peters, Thomas A.: The History and Development of Transaction Log Analysis.
In: Library Hi Tech, 11 (1993), pp. 41 - 66.

Seymour, Sharon: Online Public Access Catalog User Studies: A Review of Research Methodologies, March 1986 - November 1989.
In: Library and Information Science Research, 13 (1991), pp. 89 - 102.

Tillotson, Joy: Is Keyword Searching the Answer?
In: College and Research Libraries, 56 (1995), pp. 199 - 206

9. Acquisition Speed

Definition: The time period between the day a title (monograph) is published and the day it arrives at the library, is called acquisition speed. Acquisition speed can be split up into two aspects:

- *Ordering speed:* The time period between the day a title is published and the day it is ordered by the library

- *Delivering speed:* The time period between the day the library orders the title and the day it arrives at the library.

Aims: This indicator determines the library's promptness to react on the publication of a document as well as the vendor's quickness in delivering the ordered document. Analysing the acquisition speed helps to find out why there is a delay in providing documents and how this process can be speeded up. The indicator helps to evaluate the performance of the publisher/warehouse by analysing the delay in providing booksellers with newly published documents, and the performance of the vendor in quickly and reliably providing the documents ordered by the library. Not only the performance of the vendor is at issue, but also the performance of the library. If the library is very slow in ordering new books, the ordering speed must be improved. Only if a document is ordered early enough to be delivered by the vendor directly after its publication, can the library service for the user in regard to acquisition speed be called satisfactory. Ordering speed is the part of acquisition speed that the library itself can influence quickly and efficiently.

Comparisons between libraries in regard to acquisition speed require careful consideration of subject areas and the percentage of foreign book production of the documents in the sample. Useful results can be expected from a comparison of vendors among different libraries.

Method: First of all, a sample of publishers in different fields of research literature is chosen. They must be able and willing to provide the exact date of publication for their book production over a certain period of time (e.g. 6 months). On the international scale it might be easier for a wholesaler to provide the data for the foreign book production.

Then we determine a sample of the publishers' production within the period in question. It should include only monographs of current research literature bought by the library.

Certain types of titles should be excluded from measuring the acquisition speed, because of their particular process of publication and ordering:

- Legal deposit
- Periodicals
- Titles acquired as part of an approval plan or standing order (for those titles, only the delivering speed can be measured)

- Unordered copies delivered by the vendor's initiative
- Gifts and exchange.

The acquisition speed should only be determined for the usual procedure of ordering. Special ways of ordering like rush orders or multiple copies for the textbook collection, etc. should be examined separately.

Sample: Studies of vendor performance are based on samples of 300 to 400 titles. The sample should mirror the library's acquisition profile, e.g. in regard to foreign literature.

Collection of data: The publisher is asked to provide the exact day of publication for each title in the sample.

It may be necessary to come to terms with each publishing house as to what it regards as "day of publication". A book can be available as soon as the printer has delivered the volumes to the publisher. It is preferable to define the day of publication as the day the book is ready to be delivered by the publisher to the dealers.

In order to check the acquisition speed for foreign publications one can either contact the publishing house directly or make use of wholesalers cataloguing books and distributing notification slips. Either the wholesalers know exactly the day of publication or they can guarantee that they catalogue a book within a certain period (e.g. 1 week) after its publication.

For each title the day of publication is known for, the order file of the library is checked in regards to:

- Day of ordering
- Day of receipt
- Name of the vendor.

Calculation: We have to distinguish between the titles that have been ordered before they were ready for delivery and those that have been ordered after they were delivered.

In the case of titles ordered before the date of publication, *acquisition speed* is calculated by counting the days (including weekends) between the date of publication and the date of receipt. The total number of days is divided by the number of titles in the sample.

For titles that have been ordered after the date of publication we calculate the average *ordering speed* by counting the days between the date of publication and the date of ordering as well as the average *delivering speed* by counting the days between the date of ordering and the date of receipt. By adding the ordering speed to the delivering speed, we calculate the average *acquisition speed*.

Interpretation and possible solutions: Possible reasons for the delay in acquiring a title are:

- The library reacts too slowly to the publication of relevant titles.
- The library is too slow in processing the orders, or in claiming overdue orders.
- Publishers' delivery to the vendors is too slow.
- Vendor performance is not as good as it could be.

Solutions might be:

- Faster turnover in the use of advertising material and bibliographies (with special emphasis on cataloguing in publication)
- Making use of other means of information and processing, e.g. pre-publication announcements; online ordering; approval plans, etc.
- Improving the claiming of overdue books
- Change of vendor.

Of special interest are those titles that need longer than a reasonable delivery period. They are examined more closely in order to find possible reasons for the unusual delay.

Further reading:

Barker, Joseph W.: Random Vendor Assignment in Vendor Performance Evaluation.
In: Library Acquisitions: Practice and Theory, 10 (1986), pp. 265 - 280.

Boekhorst, Peter te; Roswitha Poll: Beschaffungsgeschwindigkeit: Leistungsmessung auf dem Gebiet der Erwerbung.
In: Bibliotheken, Service für die Zukunft / 5. Dt. Bibliothekskongreß, 83. Deutscher Bibliothekartag in Leipzig 1993. Hartwig Lohse (Ed.). - Frankfurt/Main : Klostermann, 1994 (Zeitschrift für Bibliothekswesen und Bibliographie : Sonderheft ; 58), pp. 123 - 137.

Brownson, Charles W.: A Method for Evaluating Vendor Performance.
In: Acquisitions Librarian, 5 (1991), pp. 37 - 51.

Gordon, Janet L: Measuring Supplier Performance.
In: Library Acquisitions: Theory and Practice, 18 (1994), pp. 67-70.

* **Guide to performance evaluation of library materials vendors** / Ed. by the Management and Development Committee and the Aquisitions Committee, Resources Section, Resources and Technical Services Division, American Library Association. - Chicago: American Library Association, 1988.

Lawson, Clinton D.: Where in Hell Are the Books We Ordered?: A Study of Speed of Service from Canadian Publishers.
In: Ontario Library Review, 55 (1971), pp. 237 - 241.

Miller, Ruth H.; Martha W. Niemeyer: Vendor Performance: A Study of Two Libraries.
In: Library Resources and Technical Services, 30 (1986), S. 60 - 68.

* **O'Neill, Ann:** Evaluating the Success of Acquisitions Departments: A Literature Overview.
In: Library Acquisitions, 16 (1992), pp. 209 - 219.

10. Book Processing Speed

Definition: The time period between the day a document arrives at the library and the day it is available on the shelf and/or in the catalogue is called book processing speed. This indicator determines how well the library has organized its working processes.

Aims: Analysing the book processing speed helps to find out if and where there is a delay in making new documents available for the users. The measure aims at finding out if there is a considerable delay in handling the books and if so, how to eliminate it.

The possibility of comparing different libraries depends on the degree of similarity between their processing procedures as for example the degree of automation and the use of shared cataloguing.

Method: Apart from the usual way a document is processed, there might be special procedures, which should be analysed separately:

- Rush processing procedures
- Monographs coming into the library as gifts or by exchange
- Legal deposit
- Special collections
- Documents placed in a special location.

It might also be interesting to analyse the book processing speed for each subject.

A random sample of 400 documents should be enough to determine the book processing speed.

Collection of data: Unless you can rely on a fully automated library system, which provides the necessary data automatically, each monograph gets a flag on which the different processing departments are listed:

- Acquisition
- Cataloguing
- Subject cataloguing
- Bindery preparation division
- Finishing division
- Bookstack management.

Each processing department is asked to write down on the flag the exact date after handling the document. At the end there is a sequence of dates beginning with the day the vendor delivered the title at the library and, depending on the particular conditions , ending with the day the book was placed on the shelf.

In most libraries, especially in libraries with an OPAC, the document is earlier in the catalogue than on the shelf. Therefore, the date of actual accessibility is determined by the date the document is shelved. It might be the other way round in the case of microfiche catalogues, which are produced in certain intervals, and card catalogues, where there would be some delay in filing the cards. In these cases the date when the title can be found in the catalogue should be regarded as the date of accessibility.

It has also to be taken into account whether a document has to be sent to a bindery.

Calculation: We determine the **book processing speed** by counting the days (including weekends) between the arrival date and the date the document is available on the shelf and/or in the catalogue. We do this for each of the procedures mentioned above. The total number of days needed for processing the documents in the sample is divided by the number of documents in the sample.

Interpretation and possible solutions: Possible reasons for the delay in processing books are:

- Processing procedures badly organised, e.g. wrong sequence of procedures
- Stockpiling documents before forwarding them to the next department
- Overload.

Solutions might be:

- Streamlining processing procedures
- Passing on the workload at the end of each day to the next department
- Eliminating backlogs by more flexible assignment of employees
- Making use of shared cataloguing, or buying cataloguing data.

Further reading:

Boekhorst, Peter te; Roswitha Poll: Beschaffungsgeschwindigkeit: Leistungsmessung auf dem Gebiet der Erwerbung.
In: Bibliotheken, Service für die Zukunft / 5. Dt. Bibliothekskongreß, 83. Deutscher Bibliothekartag in Leipzig 1993. Hartwig Lohse (Ed.). - Frankfurt/Main: Klostermann, 1994 (Zeitschrift für Bibliothekswesen und Bibliographie: Sonderheft ; 58), pp. 123 - 137.

Johnson, Steven D.: Rush Processing.
In: Journal of Academic Librarianship, 11 (1985), pp. 345 - 348.

Leonard, Lawrence E.: Centralised Book Processing : A Feasibility Study Based on Colorado Academic Libraries / Leonard E. Lawrence; Joan M. Maier; Richard M. Dougherty. - Metuchen, N.J.: Scarecrow Pr., 1969, esp. pp. 9 - 88.

Page, Mary; Melinda A. Reagor: Library Processing Practices by Discipline : Are Some Books More Equal than Others?
In: Library Resources and Technical Services, 38 (1994), pp. 161 - 167.

11. Availability

Definition: Availability deals with the balance of supply and demand of library materials. It is defined as the proportion of the material requested by the user that can be used in the library (including copying) or taken home immediately.

Documents that must be retrieved from closed stacks are also counted as immediately available, even if the procedure takes some time.

Aims: Analysing availability aims at finding out to what extent the library provides the users with the documents they are looking for.

It helps to analyse whether

- the titles in the collection have been chosen according to the users' needs
- there is an adequate supply of multiple copies of heavily used items
- shelving is accurate
- all acquired items have also been catalogued
- the catalogues are easy to use (see also catalogue quality, especially indicator "Known-Item-Search").

Availability is a very important indicator of any library's performance because the users' judgement of the library is based to a large extent on the availability of items they are looking for.
This indicator can be used separately for special parts of the collection, e.g. subject areas.

Comparisons are possible between libraries with a similar mission, that is if differences in user structure and coverage of subject areas in the collections are taken into consideration.

Method: Two types of availability can be distinguished:

❶ The user is looking for books on a special subject (subject search).

❷ The user is looking for a particular monograph or journal (known-item-search).

It is much easier to determine the availability rate with a known-item-search, because the number of books belonging to a special subject can only be estimated. *Therefore, the following description of "Availability" has been restricted to the known-item-search.*

The users approaching the catalogue are asked whether they are looking for a specific title. They are then given a questionnaire, which they need to fill in and give back before leaving the library. The results must be checked by library staff.

Calculation of sample size: 400 requests of titles have been recommended as reasonable sample size. 200 filled-in questionnaires will be needed, the average number of titles on each questionnaire being two. If you are doing a survey for the first time it is realistic to assume a response rate of 80%. In order to get 200 questionnaires it might be necessary to distribute up to 250 forms.

Design of questionnaire: The questionnaire to be filled in by the user should be adapted to the characteristic features of the library which is surveyed. A small pretest will help to find out whether all the particulars of the library have been thought of and misinterpretations of the text have been avoided. It is impossible to design a form applicable in all libraries. The form should contain:

- Information to the reader about the purpose of the survey and short explanation of how to fill in the form

- Columns for name of author/title/year of publication, for the signature of the document or the statement that the user could not find it. It might be useful to designate columns for the reader to state why he could not take home the book or did not want to do so (in-house-use; reservation; book regarded as irrelevant after browsing; etc.)

- Columns (preferably on the back side of the form) where members of staff can mark whether the item was acquired, catalogued, found in the catalogue, not on loan, found on the shelf, misplaced, actually taken home.

Gathering the data: Each user approaching the catalogues regarded in the survey is asked, whether she or he is looking for a specific title. If the answer is affirmative, the user is asked to fill in the form. Not only the distributors of the forms, but every staff member should be able to explain the why and the wherefore of the survey. Especially the people at the reference desks should be informed in detail.

Some experienced members of staff should check the legible titles: Are they in the catalogue or in the locator file? Is the title checked out? Is the title for reference only? How many copies are on the shelf list? Is the book still on the shelf?

Titles that have not been acquired should be traced bibliographically and checked again. Fragments of titles that cannot be proved in bibliographies are left out of the sample.

Calculation: In order to evaluate the quality of your library's general availability rate the following ratios based on the user survey described above should be checked:

- Ratio of acquired items to sought items
- Ratio of catalogued items to acquired items
- Ratio of found items to catalogued items
- Ratio of accessible items to found items
- Ratio of items for loan to accessible items
- Ratio of accurately shelved items to items for loan
- Ratio of located items to accurately shelved items.

(acquired items : sought items)	x	100	=	acquisition rate
(catalogued items : acquired items)	x	100	=	catalogue rate
(found items : catalogued items)	x	100	=	user catalogue failure rate
(accessible items : found items)	x	100	=	circulation rate
(items for loan : accessible items)	x	100	=	not for loan rate
(accurately shelved items : items for loan)	x	100	=	misshelving rate
(located items : accurately shelved items)	x	100	=	user shelf failure rate

Two kinds of availability are of special interest:

GENERAL AVAILABILITY

$$\frac{\text{items available for circulation and for in-house-use [copying]}}{\text{sought items}} \times 100$$

SPECIAL AVAILABILITY

$$\frac{\text{items available for circulation}}{\text{sought items}} \times 100$$

Our results are based on a sample, not on the whole population of users. In order to see in how far our sample result describes the actual situation, we must calculate 95% confidence intervals. They describe the range within which we are confident the answer lies.

For large samples the 95% confidence limit is 1.96 standard deviations away from the calculated value. The standard error is calculated by the square root of the formula

$$\frac{\text{percentage value x (100 - percentage value)}}{\text{number of items in the sample}}$$

If you multiply the calculated standard error by 1.96 and add this to as well as subtract it from the measured percentage value you know the 95% confidence levels of the measured value. For example, if your availability rate is 60%, based on a sample of 400, the 95% confidence limits are 55.20 and 64.80.

Interpretation and possible solutions: Availability measures how many of the books the users are looking for can actually be used in the library or taken home. The different failure rates imply the various causes for low availability. The method is somewhat time-consuming, but well worth the effort, since it provides detailed information for possible management decisions. If you find out that availability in your library is low, check the different aspects influencing availability to determine which of them needs special attention. Some ways to enhance availability:

- If your acquisition rate is low, your library's collection does not meet the demands of the users. What the user wants depends on the kind of research done in the faculties and what is taught there. Ask for checklists of the relevant literature.

- A low catalogue rate can only be improved by speeding up the time for a book to be processed. Check the process from accession department to finishing division. (see indicator "Book Processing Speed")

- In case the user catalogue failure rate severely affects your availability, the catalogue situation may be too difficult for the user, e.g. too many different catalogues (online, microfiches, cards) covering different periods and based on different cataloguing rules. Sometimes better signposting might improve the situation; in other cases comprehensive user instruction is the only solution. (See indicator "Known-Item-Search")

- The problem of a low availability because of a large number of books already on loan, can be solved either by reducing the loan period or by buying further copies. The disadvantage of the first solution is a higher workload because of the increasing circulation transactions, while the second proposal is expensive.

● A high misshelving rate can be diminished by speeding up and improving the accuracy of the shelving procedure. There may also be security problems (users steal or intentionally misplace books).

● If your availability rate is low because users do not find the accurately shelved books, try to improve the signposting in open access areas.

Because of the far-reaching consequences of some of the proposals to enhance the availability rate, some decisions should be taken only after several test periods. This is also advisable because of evident variations depending on the sampling period.

For the interpretation of the availability rate user expectation has to be considered. High expectations would lower the rate, because users would hope to find highly specific material in the library. On the other hand, low user expectations could result in a higher rate.

Further reading:

Boekhorst, Peter te: Methoden der Leistungsmessung in Bibliotheken: die Durchführung einer Verfügbarkeitsstudie an der UB Münster.
In: Bibliothek. Forschung und Praxis, 16 (1992), pp. 153 - 161.

Buckland, Michael K.: Book Availabiblity and the Library User. - New York: Pergamon Press, 1975.

Ciliberti, Anne C.: Material Availability: A Study of Academic Library Performance.
In: College and Research Libraries, 48 (1987), pp. 513 - 527.

Jacobs, N.A.; R.C. Young: Measuring Book Availability in an Academic Library: A Methodological Comparison.
In: Journal of Documentation, 51 (1995), pp. 281 - 290.

* **Kantor, Paul B.:** Objective Performance Measures for Academic and Research Libraries. - Washington, D.C.: Association of Research Libraries, 1984.

Kendrick, Curtis L.: Performance Measures of Shelving Accuracy.
In: Journal of Academic Librarianship, 17 (1991), pp. 16 - 18.

Kilgour, Frederick G.: Toward 100 Percent Availability.
In: Library Journal, 15 (1989), pp. 50 - 53.

Lapèlerie, François: L'Évaluation d'une Bibliothèque par la Méthode de Kantor.
In: Bulletin des Biliothèques de France, 39 (1994), pp. 55 - 66.

Mitchell, Eugene S.; Marie L. Radford; Judith L. Hegg: Book Availability: Academic Library
Assessment.
In: College and Research Libraries, 55 (1994), pp. 47 - 55.

* Mansbridge, John: Availability Studies in Libraries.
In: Library and Information Science Research, 8 (1986), pp. 299 - 314.

Revill, Don H.: "Availability" as a Performance Measure for Academic Libraries.
In: Journal of Librarianship, 19 (1987), pp. 14 - 30.

Rashid, Haseeb F.: Book Availability as a Performance Measure of a Library: An Analysis of
the Effectiveness of a Health Science Library.
In: Journal of the American Society for Information Science, 41 (1990), pp. 501 - 507.

12. Document Delivery Time

Definition: Document delivery determines the average time between the moment a user starts with the necessary procedures to borrow a document and the moment the item is checked out or available at the issue desk. The indicator should only be applied for delivery procedures within the library. It is not suited for assessing the quality of delivering documents from other libraries (see indicator no. 13 "Interlibrary Loan Speed") or document supply centres.

Aims: Checking document delivery regularly helps to spot and obviate difficulties that prevent the user from getting the documents in the shortest time possible.

The indicator provides valuable information for all libraries, whether they have open access to the collection or large parts of the collection in closed stacks. Comparisons are possible between similarly structured libraries, however, local differences in regard to means of transportation, design, and construction of the library building, etc. need to be considered.

Method: The best way to check document delivery is to select a number of test subjects, who are known to be regular users of the library and can be expected to be familiar with the basic procedures. Students employed as temporary help seem to be suitable persons for this test.

Collection of data: The first step is to choose the documents the test subjects will be looking for. A random sample of 35 to 50 titles from the open stacks, as well as 35 to 50 titles from the closed stacks, will provide reliable results. Each test person should not be given more than 10 titles, because the search strategy might become a routine and the results no longer be representative. The collection of data should be spread equally over the day to avoid the results being unduly affected by peak times. This correlation should also influence the choice of the test period.

Before the bibliographical description of each title is given to the testee, it must be guaranteed that the volumes in question are available and in their proper place on the shelf.

The testee is given one form at a time.

● For titles to be retrieved from the *closed stacks*, the form contains the following details:

- The title of the document
- Starting time
- End of catalogue search
- Time of filling in order form
- Time of the document being available at the issue desk.

● For titles to be retrieved from the *open stacks*, the form contains the following details:

- The title of the document
- Starting time
- End of catalogue search
- Time of the document checked out at the issue desk.

There should be columns to fill in the exact time of day (hours, mins. and secs.) at each measuring time and a place to write down the signature of the document in question as a proof that the testee found the right title.

Document Delivery Time Form
(CLOSED STACKS)

date:

Title:

Shelf mark:

❶ starting time: _ _ : _ _ : _ _

❷ end of catalogue search: _ _ : _ _ : _ _

❸ order form filled in: _ _ : _ _ : _ _

❹ book available at issue desk: _ _ : _ _ : _ _

The test subjects are given stop-watches to record the time from the start (identical starting point near the catalogue) until the last measuring point is reached. There is the problem with books from the closed stacks that the time of their arrival at the issue desk cannot be taken down by the testees. One of the staff members working at the issue desk should be given a list of the titles ordered by the testees and asked to write down the exact time the user could have collected the document. All the documents should be brought to the person supervising the document delivery test in order to rule out any mistakes by the testee or the library staff.

Calculation: For each title in the sample we calculate the average time for each category measured. Then we could say, for example, that on the average, users spent 3 mins.15 secs. looking up a title in the catalogue. Having calculated the average for the documents in each group (open stacks, closed stacks), it is then possible to say, for example, that it takes 7 mins. 35 secs. to fetch a document from the open stacks, or 15 mins. 21 secs. for the time from ordering a book from the closed stacks until it is available for the reader at the issue desk (both including the time for searching the catalogue).

Interpretation and possible solutions: The shorter the document delivery time is, the better the performance of the library. Reasons for delay could be:

- The users might have difficulties in finding the titles in the catalogue. Perhaps the knowledge of cataloguing rules is insufficient and user education in this respect would need be improved. Or the catalogue situation is too complicated and the differences between card, microfiche or online catalogues have to be explained in detail. Maybe handling the OPAC is too difficult. (See indicator "Known-Item-Search")

- If it takes definitely too much time for the reader to find the book on the open shelves, the shelving system might be too complicated. If that cannot be changed, one should think of measures to facilitate the user's orientation, e.g. by improving the signposting.

- Delays in fetching the documents from the closed stacks may arise from forwarding the order forms too slowly or the number of stack assistants being too small. In this case the number of staff members working in the stacks should be increased or, if possible, closed stacks should be opened so that the users can fetch their books themselves.

Further Reading:

Dougherty, R. M.: The Evaluation of Campus Library Document Delivery Service. In: College and Research Libraries, 34 (1973), pp. 29 - 39.

* Kantor, Paul B.: Objective Performance Measures for Academic and Research Libraries. - Washington, D.C.: Association of Research Libraries, 1984, esp. pp. 25 - 41.

* Orr, Richard H. and A. P. Schless: Document Delivery Capabilities of Major Biomedical Libraries in 1968: Results of a National Survey Employing Standardized Tests. In: Bulletin of the Medical Library Association, 60 (1972), pp. 382 - 422.

Orr, Richard H., Vern M. Pings; Irwin H. Pizer; Edwin E. Olson; Carol C. Spencer: Development of Methodologic Tools for Planning and Managing Library Services: II. Measuring a Library's Capability for Providing Documents. In: Bulletin of the Medical Library Association, 56 (1968), pp. 241 - 267.

13. Interlibrary Loan Speed

Definition: The effectiveness of document supply by way of interlibrary loans can be described by various indicators, for example speed, coverage and costs. Although costs obviously need to be taken into account, it is suggested that the primary indicator be the success rate, which is defined as the proportion (%) of documents requested through local and international interlibrary loans that are supplied (availability) within a certain period of time, say 7, 14, 21 and 21+ days.

Aims: A major function of any library and information organization is to supply documents to meet the needs of the users. The extent to which a library is able to do this successfully depends on the quality and range of its collections, the availability of documents in the collections when needed, and the facilities to obtain documents elsewhere if not available in the library. To this end, libraries must monitor and evaluate not only the success rate of users finding documents available on the shelf at the time of the request (see indicator "Availability") but also the success rate for documents obtained from other libraries, nationally as well as internationally.

The aim of an interlending service as part of the document supply function of a library, is to obtain required material not owned by the library, from other libraries. It is, therefore, desirable that procedures be developed in order to monitor the effectiveness of obtaining material from other sources. It is furthermore essential that these procedures be standardized to enable libraries to compare their results. The establishment of a success rate as the critical performance indicator should make this possible and will simultaneously serve as encouragement for librarians to improve their standards.

The indicator is of interest to all libraries offering interlibrary lending services.

Method: Depending on various factors, for instance, size and location of the library, staff time available, etc, a decision will firstly have to be made regarding the duration of the survey. Three possibilities may be considered:

❶ The measurement could be conducted on a continuous basis. The results are calculated at monthly, quarterly and annual intervals. This method enables the library to detect problems as soon as they occur and to take corrective action.

❷ The measurement could be conducted only once to determine a library's success rate. The problem with this possibility is that the success rate cannot be monitored.

❸ The measurement could be conducted at pre-determined intervals. This method may be preferred since the surveys could be carried out during less busy periods. Although the sample size will vary according to the survey population, it is recommended that at least 100 items be included for a rough indication, and about 300/400 for a fairly accurate figure. The total number of items requested annually could serve as a basis for the calculation of the length and frequencies of the surveys.

The following steps should be followed when conducting an interlibrary loan (ILL) survey:

- The purpose and procedures of the survey should be stated clearly.

- The implementation date should be set (it is generally best to collect data from items received in a concentrated timespan of a week or two).

- The staff who will be directly concerned with the survey should be well informed of the purpose and the procedures.

- The sample size should be determined.

- The log sheets needed (manual or computerised) should be prepared.

Collection of data: Each request should be coded in such a way that the required information can be transferred to a log sheet once the transaction is concluded. For this purpose the following dates must be entered on the interlending record:

- The date the user submits the request
- The date the document is ordered on ILL
- The date of receipt of the document.

Calculation: The number of days between the date the user submitted the request and the ordering date of the document on ILL must be calculated and entered on the log sheet. The number of days represents the time taken by ILL staff to process the request (A).

The number of days between the ordering and receipt of the document must also be calculated and entered on the log sheet. The number of days represents the time required by the supplying library to process the request as well as postal time.

The total number of days pertaining to the request is calculated by the addition of the times already calculated (C). (A + B = C)

(It must be pointed out that essentially only the time from the date the user submits the request until receipt of the document is taken into consideration. It is, however, useful to divide this period as described above in order to establish where delays are occurring.)

The log sheet also needs to make provision for the period specified (one week, two weeks, etc. as may apply to the specific library) in order to establish the success rate for each of those periods. For this purpose, it needs to indicate how many documents were received within each of the specified periods. Calculations can be made by considering only the number of days from when the document was requested until it was received (B), which will provide a measure for the response time of supplying libraries. Alternatively the measure may be calculated on the total number of days involved (C).

Log sheet

Request received	Ordered ILL	Days (A)	Document Received	Days (B)	Total days (C)	Periods			
						-7	-14	-21	+21

Example 1: Calculation of measurement pertaining to (B) time:

Request received	Ordered ILL	Days (A)	Document Received	Days (B)	Total days (C)	Periods (days)			
						-7	-14	-21	+21
07/02/94	08/02/94	1	15/02/94	7	8	1			
10/02/94	10/02/94	0	15/02/94	5	5	1			
02/02/94	04/02/94	2	16/02/94	12	14		1		
31/01/94	01/02/94	1	16/02/94	15	16			1	
28/01/94	31/01/94	3	17/02/94	17	20			1	
27/01/94	28/01/94	1	22/02/94	25	26				1
Total						2	1	2	1

Example 2: Calculation of measurement pertaining to (C) time:

Request received	Ordered ILL	Days (A)	Document Received	Days (B)	Total days (C)	Periods (days) -7	-14	-21	+21
07/02/94	08/02/94	1	15/02/94	7	8		1		
10/02/94	10/02/94	0	15/02/94	5	5	1			
02/02/94	04/02/94	2	16/02/94	12	14		1		
31/01/94	01/02/94	1	16/02/94	15	16			1	
28/01/94	31/01/94	3	17/02/94	17	20			1	
27/01/94	28/01/94	1	22/02/94	25	26				1
Total						1	2	2	1

Results from example 1:

1. 33,3% supplied by other libraries within 7 days.

2. 50,0% supplied by other libraries within 14 days.

3. 83,3% supplied by other libraries within 21 days.

Results from example 2:

1. 16,7% supplied by other libraries within 7 days.

2. 50,0% supplied by other libraries within 14 days.

3. 83,3% supplied by other libraries within 21 days.

Interpretation and possible solutions: With the help of this indicator the library can find out deficiencies in handling ILL requests. If the average number of days (A) is too high, the requests must be processed more quickly. Either an increase in staff might be the solution, or more efficient ways of checking the users' bibliographical data and the holdings of other libraries, e.g. union catalogues in machine-readable form. If the average number of days (B) is too high, there is little one can do to speed up processing time in the library that provides the document. If the postal service turns out to be extremely bad one could think of establishing a book van service. In that case, the interlibrary loan speed could thereby be improved considerably, provided that the region covered by the service contains a fairly large number of libraries which are not too far apart.

In regards to speeding up the delivery of the documents, the most significant changes are to be expected to come in the near future. New communication technologies will improve ILL considerably. Instead of sending one book or photocopy by post or book van from one library to the other, the contents of the book or article will be transmitted via an electronic document delivery service. The whole procedure described above can easily be adapted to the changed circumstances. Instead of being counted in days the delay could be measured in hours.

Further Reading:

* Kantor, Paul B.: Objective Performance Measures for Academic and Research Libraries. - Washington, D.C.: Association of Research Libraries, 1984, esp. pp. 57-73.

Library Performance Measurement: Ansvarsbibliotekenes undersøkelse av fjernkopitjenesten / Styringsgruppen for Ansvarsbibliotek i Norge. - Oslo. Universitetsbibliotekets trykkeri, 1993. - 39 p. - (Skrifter fra Riksbiblioteksjenesten ; 63)

Waldhart, Thomas J.: Performance Evaluation of Interlibrary Loan in the United States: A Review of Research.
In: Library and Information Science Research, 7 (1985), pp. 313 - 331.

Willemse, John: Improving Interlending Through Goalsetting and Performance Measurement.
In: Interlending and Document Supply, 21 (1993), pp. 13 - 17.

14. Correct Answer Fill Rate

Definition: This indicator defines the proportion of test questions which are correctly answered by the reference service.

Reference questions for this indicator should be a query for a short, factual, unambiguous answer that can easily be evaluated as correct or incorrect. Possible "shades of grey" in regards to the degree of correctness or completeness should be avoided as much as possible or categorized beforehand. Asking for directions (e.g. where to find a specific bibliograhy) is not regarded as a reference question.

Aims: A library and information institution is categorized as a service organisation whose primary goal it is to provide quality services to its clients. Whilst the reference service is a key aspect in most libraries, it is also recognised that it is an expensive service to provide because of the professional staff component and the availability of and access to a vast array of expensive bibliographic sources (print/non-print; local/decentralized). For this reason, it is important for reference services to be evaluated using both quantitative and qualitative methods.

This indicator judges the quality of reference transactions in terms of accurateness and completeness of the supplied information. The indicator also has some disadvantages:

- It does not quantify the workload of the library's information service.
- It reduces the complexity of the reference transaction to correctly or incorrectly answered factual questions.
- It does not tell us anything about the user's perceptions of the transaction output/outcome.

This last point can be resolved by determining the user satisfaction level with the reference service as described by indicator no. 16 "User Satisfaction", relating the librarian's actual performance and the user's expectations.

Surveys have shown that reference librarians answer approximately 55% of the questions received, completely and accurately. The correct answer fill rate is an indispensable indicator to find out the reasons for this not very satisfying result, and to devise methods on how to improve this key component of overall quality of the reference service.

The indicator is useful to all libraries offering reference and information services. The performance of libraries can be compared by this indicator, provided that

- an identical list of questions and answers is used
- local differences in staffing are taken into account
- there are similar reference collections.

Method: The correct answer fill rate is measured by unobtrusive testing. The reference staff as a whole is tested, not the single individual. To avoid moral objections of staff members, the test should be strictly anonymous. Collaboration with staff representatives might be useful. A set of representative questions is compiled. The reference staff are asked unobtrusively to answer the questions. Their answers are evaluated and rated. Optionally, the time needed to provide the answer is recorded. Finally, the proportion of correct answers provided (within a certain period of time) can be determined.

The choice of the questions is very important. To be easily evaluated, they must be short, factual and unambiguous. The list should be representative of the variety of questions asked at the reference desk. Furthermore, the questions should fit the special circumstances of the institution and the library in question. Otherwise, the results will not be relevant for the library. However, that makes it difficult to copy questions from one of the numerous unobtrusive tests in other libraries. It must be guaranteed that the questions can be answered with the help of the reference collection at the disposal of the staff, including e.g. access to databases..

The number of questions to be asked depends on the size of the reference department. Three to five questions per staff member will lead to a fairly representative picture of the reference department's performance. In small libraries, where only three or four people are in charge of the reference service, the number per staff member can be higher.

The questions must be pretested. This helps to prevent ambiguities which might influence the result of the survey and to decide the different options which allow a question to be categorized as correct or incorrect.

The questioning should be spread over various days and times of day to include peak times as well as times with less use.

Collection of data: As soon as a representative set of questions has been pretested it is submitted to the reference department by surrogate users who visit the library personally, or who indirectly contact the library via telephone, letter or electronic mail.

Surrogate users have to be trained in order to guarantee the unobtrusiveness of the measurement process. The interaction between reference librarian and user should be as normal as possible, therefore surrogate users must be convincing. They must learn how to record carefully the outcome as well as the time used, when the interview is over. Student assistants seem to be very suitable for this task. The surrogate users should not write down the name of the person they have asked.

An important point is what is expected as an answer to the question. Basically, there are two ways of answering questions:

> ❶ telling the users what they want to know
> ❷ telling them where in the reference collection they can
>   find the answer themselves.

The quality of a library's reference service is easier to evaluate on the basis of the actual answers. But if the user has been directed to the right material to find an answer, the answer should be counted as correct.

Indirect contact by telephone or mail is usually less typical of the interview situation in academic libraries, but has the advantage that the user is told the answer instead of where to find it. Furthermore, indirect contact can be arranged with less effort. Especially in the case of telephone questions the number of surrogate users can be considerably smaller. There is less danger of arousing the librarian's suspicion. The surrogate users need to be trained what to say if the librarian tries to pinpoint the question. In order to record the outcome of the interview they should use a log sheet as shown below (It shows the answers to two questions. Q1: Is the catalogue of Utrecht University Library available on the Internet? Q2: When was Ludwik H. Morstin's comedy Obrona Ksantypy performed for the first time?)

Although accuracy and completeness are the main evaluation criteria, the time the librarian needs to answer the question also helps to determine the quality of reference service. It must be taken into account that it usually takes more time to provide the user with a complete answer than to refer him to a title in the reference collection. To record the time between asking the question and receiving the answer via telephone or mail has some inaccuracies. If the librarian has to call back there are several reasons for delay. That is also the case if the answer is sent via mail or email.

Calculation: The number of correct answers is divided by the total number of questions that have been asked. The result is multiplied by 100.

● Correct answer = fully correct; all aspects covered; user referred to the right sources

● Incorrect answer = simply wrong; only partially correct; not all aspects covered; no answer at all (librarian too busy; user asked to call or return later; user referred to another library.

Qu. No.	Answer	Score	Time Start hh:mm	Time End hh:mm	Time Total hh:mm
1	Yes	corr.	14:53	14:56	00:03
2	1954	incorr.	09:12	09:17	00:05

If more complicated questions have been used in the list, a more differentiated way of scoring should be used. A possible subdivision of answers could be:

● Fully correct (or: users sent to sources which provided the correct answer)
● Almost correct; most aspects covered

- Partly correct; not all aspects covered
- Partly incorrect (or: users sent to inappropriate sources)
- Simply wrong; no answer at all.

(For an example of differentiated scoring see Elzy and Lancaster cited below.)

Interpretation and possible solutions: The factors affecting the reference process are manifold: the reference librarian, the user, the question, the reference collection. Combined with the fact that we are dealing with a product of human interaction, it is very difficult to establish a clearcut relationship between cause and effect. It also needs to be considered that, in spite of pretesting questions and answers, the decision whether the answer is counted as correct or incorrect may be subjective.

A low proportion of correct answers points to the following aspects:

- Gaps in the reference collection
- Insufficient knowledge of the existing reference works
- Lack of communication skills
- Insufficient staffing of the reference desk.

More detailed information about the reasons could be gained from

- having the surrogate users note down the procedures followed for answering the question, e.g. which sources were checked, or whether the user was asked to explain the question
- conducting a user satisfaction survey with special emphasis on reference service.

It must be emphasized that the indicator "Correct Answer Fill Rate" covers just a small, but nevertheless very important part of the reference process.

Further Reading:

Childers, Thomas: The Quality of Reference: Still Moot After 20 Years.
In: Journal of Academic Librarianship, 13 (1987), pp. 73 - 74.

*Elzy, Chery; Alan Nourie; F.W. Lancaster; Kurt M. Joseph: Evaluating Reference Service in a Large Academic Library.
In: College and Research Libraries, 52 (1991), pp. 454 - 465.

* Hernon, Peter; Charles R. McClure: Unobtrusive Testing and Library Reference Services. Norwood, NJ: Ablex, 1987.

Jardine, Carolyn W.: Maybe the 55 Percent Rule Doesn't Tell the Whole Story: A User-Satisfaction Survey.
In: College and Research Libraries, 56 (1995), pp. 477 - 485.

* Lancaster, F. W.: If You Want to Evaluate Your Library. - 2nd ed. - Champaign, Ill.: Graduate School of Library and Information Science, 1993, pp. 151 - 180.

Murfin, M. E.: Evaluation of Reference Service by User Report of Success.
In: Reference Librarian, 49/50 (1995), pp. 229 - 241.

Schmidt, Janine: Reference Performance in College Libraries.
In: Australian Academic and Research Libraries, 11 (1980), pp. 87 - 95.

Williams, R.: An Unobtrusive Survey of Academic Library Reference Services.
In: Library and Information Research News, 10 (1987), pp. 12 - 40.

15. Remote Uses per Capita

Definition: This indicator relates the number of remote uses by members of the primary user group during a year to the primary user group.

In regards to this indicator, remote use is defined as use of the services offered by the library on the electronic network (e.g. OPAC, CD-ROM databases, electronic publications, general information etc.) from access points outside the library or its branch libraries. It does not include telephone calls or requests by fax.

Aims: This indicator determines the extent that the library's services available for remote access are used by the primary user group.
Only highly automated libraries with similar network systems that provide adequate statistical information can be compared.

Method: The method depends on the statistics of the network system.

Method 1: For this method, the network statistics must keep track of all user transactions and must be able to distinguish between access points

- inside the library (including branch libraries)
- outside the library, but belonging to the institution's network
- outside the institution's network.

The remote uses by terminals outside the library, but belonging to the institution's network, are counted as remote uses by members of the institution. Remote uses on private terminals by members of the institution are excluded.

Every log-on to a service offered by the library is counted as one remote use, irrespective of transaction type (specific searches, HELP-commands, downloading etc.).

Calculation: The number of remote uses by members of the institution (as defined above) per year is divided by the number of members of the institution.

Method 2: An E-mail questionnaire is offered to a sample of remote users asking for

- status of the user (member of the institution?)
- target group (e.g. undergraduate, faculty staff, etc.)

If the target group is asked for, the indicator can be subdivided by target group, e.g.

- remote uses per faculty staff

This method includes remote uses on private terminals by members of the institution.

104

Calculation: The sample is extrapolated to provide the total number of remote uses per year by members of the institution. This number is divided by the number of members of the institution.

Both methods could be used to determine remote use of specific services, e.g.

- OPAC
- CD-ROM databases
- document delivery services.

In method 1, this would require that the network statistics can separate transactions by the services used.

In method 2, the E-mail questionnaire must ask for the type of service that has been used.

Interpretation and possible solutions: The indicator should be applied regularly in order to show changes over time in reagrds to remote use of the library services.

Low numbers could point to

- lack of marketing of library services
- insufficient help screens
- difficulties in accessing the system
- unattractive choice of services (e.g. CD-ROM).

An electronic satisfaction survey could help to define causes for low remote use (see indicator no. 17 "User Satisfaction with Services Offered for Remote Use"). High numbers, proving the attractiveness of the electronic services, could suggest widening the services and would help decision-making for allocating resources to this sector.

The indicator does not show the proportion of the primary user group who are active remote users, as one person can have used the system many times. To be able to show that, would require differentiation of remote use by individual, not only by individual terminals. Another way of assessing active remote users would be to send out a questionnaire to a sample of the primary user group.

Further reading:

McClure, Charles R.; Cynthia Lopato: Performance Measures for the Academic Networked Environment.
In: Proceedings of the 1st Northumbria International Conference on Performance Measurement in Libraries and Information Services / Edited Pat Wressell. - Newcastle upon Tyne: Information North, 1995, pp. 63 - 73.

16. User Satisfaction

Note: Two levels of user satisfaction can be measured:

❶ General user satisfaction which evaluates the services of the library as a whole.

❷ User satisfaction with individual services or components of those services, for example, opening hours or attributes of the librarian.

Since the definition and method of determining levels of satisfaction are the same, these two levels of satisfaction are dealt with simultaneously.

Definition: User satisfaction is a subjective output measure which reflects the quality dimension of library services as a whole or specific components of the service being provided.

User satisfaction is defined as the average rating given by users on a five-point scale ranging from very unsatisfactory to very satisfactory expressing their perception of the library services as a whole or of individual services offered by the library.

Aims: A library and information institution can be categorized as a service organization whose primary goal is to provide quality services to its clients. Quality is judged ultimately in terms of effectiveness by using an evaluative process to determine the extent to that the service is achieving its goal. The effectiveness of library and information services is judged in terms of **outputs** which comprise the products and services generated by library activities.

It is increasingly recognized that, since the user is the direct recipient of a library's outputs, it is meaningful to have some form of measure that reflects the user's perceptions about the extensiveness (amount) and the effectiveness (quality) of the outputs or results received from the service. The purpose of this indicator, therefore, is to provide a practical management tool that **quantifies user satisfaction levels** as numerical scores on a satisfaction scale, in order to be able to monitor the quality of the library service as a whole or individual aspects of it.

All libraries will benefit from conducting a user satisfaction service, since it is the pivotal point of user-oriented performance measurement. Provided that identical survey forms and similar sampling procedures and periods are used, the results of user satisfaction surveys at different libraries can be compared. In the case of individual services, comparisons are only feasible when local differences in the range of service, staffing, or processing etc. are taken into account. Comparisons between libraries are made difficult by the fact that the rating of the service quality depends on the individual expectations of each user. The higher the quality of services is, that a user is familiar with, the more difficult it is to meet his or her expectations. In each questionnaire a question on the user's status (undergraduate, postgraduate, academic staff, external user) should be included so that the results of the survey can be differentiated according to specific user groups.

Method: In order to solicit opinions and perceptions of the users to determine satisfaction levels, a survey, in the form of a questionnaire, is mailed to a random sample of actual users belonging to the primary user group or to special target groups. The response rate will, however, be far better if the questionnaire is given to users as they enter or leave the library.

Collection of data: It is practical to incorporate the question about the user's overall satisfaction with the services of the library, either as part of other surveys used for performance indicators as, for example, "Availability", or as part of a survey analysing user satisfaction with specific services:

- It reduces the amount of work bound up with conducting a survey.
- In order to be sure that the users remain willing to answer questionnnaires the number of users in the sample should be kept as low as possible.

General user satisfaction

The type of question that could be used is:

Q1. Overall, how would you rate your satisfaction with the performance of the service you receive when visiting the library?

very unsatisfactory   1 ❑   2 ❑   3 ❑   4 ❑   5 ❑   very satisfactory

If 1 or 2, please comment:

The actual performance is scored by the respondent using a five-item Likert scale ranging from a weak 1 to a high 5:

value of 1	very unsatisfactory
value of 2	unsatisfactory
value of 3	moderately satisfactory
value of 4	satisfactory
value of 5	very satisfactory

If so desired, a diagnostic element can be introduced by providing an open-ended question which asks respondents to indicate why they are dissatisfied with the overall performance. Useful insights and suggestions for improvement might be gained from the comments.

User satisfaction with individual services and the librarian

Tangible results can be expected questions about the users' perception of the individual services offered by the library: opening hours; quality of lending collection, undergraduate collection, or rare book collection; lending procedures; study facilities; photocopying; reference service; user education; interlibrary lending, etc. We suggest including all questions in one questionnaire, in order to evaluate the results more efficiently. On the other hand, it seems preferable to split up the questionnaire into smaller units out of consideration for the imposed inconvenience on the sampled users and the necessity of repeating surveys in the future.

A series of specific questions that measure satisfaction with a range of dimensions associated with a major service can be also designed to provide more depth and insight into service effectiveness. For example, the dimensions of a reference and information service that could be evaluated in terms of user satisfaction include the following aspects:

- Skills and attributes of the librarian
- Bibliographic service
- Current awareness service
- Reference service collections.

Each dimension has attributes which can be measured more specifically in terms of the user satisfaction formula. For example, user satisfaction with the skills and attributes of the reference librarian can be evaluated according to

- availability
- attitude
- negotiation skills
- library service knowledge.

In order to determine the level of performance, statements can be provided with which the respondent agrees or disagrees; for example, as regards the attitude of library staff, the following statement could be used:

Q2. The reference librarian has a positive, friendly and courteous attitude.

strongly disagree   1 ❑   2 ❑   3 ❑   4 ❑   5 ❑   strongly agree

If 1 or 2, please comment:

The actual performance is scored by the respondent using a five-item Likert scale ranging from a weak 1 to a high 5:

value of 1	strongly disagree (very poor performance)
value of 2	disagree (poor performance)
value of 3	moderately agree (acceptable performance)
value of 4	agree (good performance/satisfactory)
value of 5	strongly agree (very good performance)

If so desired, a diagnostic element can be introduced by providing an open-ended question which asks respondents to indicate why they are dissatisfied with the skills dimension of the reference service. This is not quantifiable but helps to identify areas requiring improvement or refinement.

Sample size: Although the sample size for surveys will vary with the survey population, it has been recommended that at least 100 forms should be obtained, a number closer to 400 is preferable.

It should be noted that mailed surveys are generally characterized by poor response rates, especially if not followed up by repeated mailings. However, this can be labour, time, and cost intensive and should be well planned in the initial stages.

If the questionnaires are handed out to the users when they enter or leave the library, the choice of the sampling period is very important to avoid seasonal peak times and to cover opening hours completely so that all user groups can voice their opinion.

Calculation: A level of satisfaction is derived by taking the sum of the scores of the actual performance as indicated by the user responses in the surveys given or sent to the sample population and dividing it by the number of persons having answered the questionnaire. Usually the questionnaire will consist of more than one question. For each question the average score is calculated.

In addition, it is informative to know how the values are distributed along the spectrum of different possible answers, for different distributions could influence the conclusions drawn from the results. It makes a difference, wether the opinions are strongly polarized or whether they are distributed normally.

Example Q1: The question concerning the overall user satisfaction is answered by 371 users: 8 consider the performance of the library very unsatisfactory; 24 regard it as unsatisfactory; 120 as moderately satisfactory; 164 as satisfactory; and 55 as very satisfactory.

```
  8   x  1   =     8
 24   x  2   =    48
120   x  3   =   360
164   x  4   =   656
 55   x  5   =   275
                1347  :   371   =   3.63
```

The average rating is 3.6.

Interpretation and possible solutions: For the interpretation of the results it is of vital importance to bear in mind that the findings are

- based on the subjective opinions of a random sample of library users
- strongly influenced by the expectations of the individual user.

If the average rating of the overall user satisfaction is lower than expected or deemed insufficient, the library must find out exactly what the users criticise the library for. Here the possibility of giving the users an opportunity to voice their criticism in detail will provide valuable information. This is also true for the results of user surveys concerning individual services. In this case ways of improvement such as initiatives in staff development suggest themselves more easily.

If satisfaction with a specific service is low, a more objective performance indicator could be used to clarify the causes of discontent, e.g. low satisfaction with the library's collection analysed in detail with the help of the indicator "Availability".

If a user satisfaction survey has asked for satisfaction with all relevant services, there will probably be more than one service with a low satisfaction rate. It makes management decisions regarding reallocation of resources easier, if, at the end of the survey, all services discussed in the survey are submitted to ranking by the users.

> **Q3.** We also want to know which services you think are the most important. Please rank the services in terms of this importance: The service you consider most important as 1, the next most important as 2, and so on. If you consider two or more services to be equally important, please give them the same ranking.

Importance	Services
	Opening hours
	Collection relevance
	Collection availability
	Reference Service
	Study facilities
	...

The degree of urgency for action needed is determined by the ranking result:

- high satisfaction and high ranking   ➡ no need for action

- high satisfaction and low ranking   ➡ action necessary if resources are needed for other services

- low satisfaction and low ranking   ➡ reaction not urgent

- low satisfaction and high ranking   ➡ immediate action necessary.

In any case, the results of user satisfaction surveys should be made known to the users and the library staff with the help of poster sessions and other forms of publication, preferably with examples of actual improvements of the service quality as a consequence of the user satisfaction survey.

Further reading:

Dalton, Gwenda M. E.: Quantitative Approach to User Satisfaction in Reference Service Evaluation.
In: Suid-Afrikaanse Tydskrif vir Biblioteek- en Inligtingkunde, 60 (1992), pp. 89 - 103.

Buch, Harald; Peter te Boekhorst: Benutzerzufriedenheit: Umfrage in der Universität- und Landesbibliothek Münster.
In: Bibliotheksdienst, 30 (1996), to be published.

Davies, Annette; Ian Kirkpatrick: To Measure Service.
In: Library Association Record, 96 (1994), pp. 88 - 89.

McCarthy, Cheryl Ann: Students' Perceived Effectiveness Using the University Library.
In: College and Research Libraries, 56 (1995), pp. 221 - 234.

Seay, Thomas; Sheila Seaman; David Cohen: Measuring and Improving the Quality of Public Services: A Hybrid Approach.
In: Library Trends, 44 (1996), pp. 464 - 490.

Wallace, Linda K.: Customer Feedback - How to Get It.
In: College and Research Libraries News, 55 (1994), pp. 64 - 65.

17. User Satisfaction with Services Offered for Remote Use

Note: User satisfaction with services offered for remote use is dealt with separately from user satisfaction with other individual services because of its growing importance. As many libraries still have to gain experience about quality issues in remote use, it seems expedient to go into more detail about this special survey.

The general method of data collection and calculation for a satisfaction survey is described in indicator no. 16 "User Satisfaction" and is not repeated here.

Definition: This indicator shows the users' rating of their satisfaction with the library's services offered for remote use.

In regards to this indicator, remote use is defined as use of the services offered by the library in the electronic network (e.g. OPAC, CD-ROM databases, electronic publications, general information etc.) from access points outside the library or its branch libraries. It does not include telephone calls or requests by fax.

Aims: To assess to what degree remote users are satisfied with the services offered.

All libraries providing remote access should make use of this indicator because it gives them a clear indication as to how far the considerable financial investment in such a service is justified. Comparisons with other libraries depend on the similarity of the network system and the range of services offered.

Method: An E-mail questionnaire is offered to a sample of remote users at the point of logging off from the service. This might be triggered by the access control software of the network. The questionnaire could ask for satisfaction with the following aspects on a five-point scale:

- Systems availability
- Stability of data communication
- Ease of logon procedures
- Ease of search procedures
- Response time
- Download and printout possibilities
- Helpfulness of help screens
- Helpfulness of librarians' assistance (during opening hours of the library)
- Range of databases and information offered.

Some of these aspects could be differentiated by the different services offered for remote use (OPAC, CD-ROM databases, electronic publications etc.).

Calculation: The sum of the performance scores is divided by the number of persons having answered the questionnaire.

112

Interpretation and possible solutions: Management decisions based on this survey will depend on what aspects of remote use show insufficient user satisfaction.

Systems availability for 24 hours a day may be difficult to achieve because of the time needed for backups and maintenance. This could be explained in the opening screen of the system.

Stability of data communication, response time, and download and printout possibilities could be dependent on network procedures for which the library is not responsible. The library will probably need constant cooperation with the institutional or local computer centre to achieve fast and reliable data-transfer.

Dissatisfaction with logon procedures would show the need for reconsidering the administration software and hardware.

Difficulties with search procedures could be obviated by combining the different procedures for the individual databases into a single, user-friendly interface with an easy to use menu.

Dissatisfaction with help screens will be easiest to deal with as remote users could be asked to point out their specific difficulties. New help screens could be devised in cooperation with users.

Low satisfaction with librarians' assistance (by E-mail or phone) could suggest further training of reference librarians in handling electronic services.

Low satisfaction with the databases and information offered for remote use would need to be seen in the context of indicators for collection building as a whole. This aspect of a remote use satisfaction survey could lead to decisions as to resource allocation, if the faculty of the remote user has been asked for (e.g. satisfaction of chemistry students with databases offered for remote use).

Further Reading:

Barbuto, Domenica M.; Elenor E. Cevallos: The Delivery of Reference Services in a CD-ROM LAN Environment: A Case Study.
In: RQ, 34 (1994), pp. 60-75.

Ferl, Terry Ellen; Larry Millsap: Remote Use of the University of California MELVYL Library System: An Online Survey.
In: Information Technology and Libraries, 11 (1992), pp. 285-303.

Kock, Marthie de: Remote Users of an Online Public Access Catalogue (OPAC): Problems and Support.
In: The Electronic Library, 11 (1993), pp. 241-243.

Millsap, Larry; Terry Ellen Ferl: Search Patterns of Remote Users: An Analysis of OPAC Transaction Logs.
In: Information Technology and Libraries, 12 (1993), pp. 321-343.

Glossaries

English Glossary

The glossary does not contain terms that are widely used in performance measurement or that are self-explaining. It is confined to terms

- that are used in a special sense in the context of these guidelines
- that have been used with a different meaning in the literature on performance measurement
- whose definition many readers might not be familiar with.

Academic library: A library forming an integral part of a college, university, or other academic institution for postsecondary education, organized and administered to meet the information needs of students, faculty, and affiliated staff of the institution.

Availability: The proportion of user searches for library materials that are successful at the time of the user's visit.

Circulation: Number of items charged out for use, usually (though not always) outside the library. Includes initial charges and renewals, general collection, and reserves.

Cost-effectiveness: Costs of achieving a particular level of effectiveness.

Degree of use: The relation between a subject's proportion of the circulation, its proportion of the annual intake, and the proportion of the annual budget spent on the subject.

Document delivery: The average time between the moment a user starts with the necessary procedures to borrow a document and the moment the item is available at the issue desk.

Effectiveness: Extent to which the library is achieving its goals and objectives.

Efficiency: Relation between resources input and resulting outputs.

Facilities: Space and equipment available to library users.

Fill rate: Proportion of searches, requests, or questions that are successful.

Goal: The fundamental state of affairs that is intended to be reached and that is formulated to last over a longer time.

In-house materials use: The number of documents used in the library but not charged out.

Inputs: Resources used by the library.

Library visits: Number of user visits to the library in terms of number of people entering the library, including people attending activities, meetings, and those requiring no staff services.

Management: Utilizing material and human resources to accomplish designated goals.

Market penetration: The proportion of the library's potential users who actually use the library.

Measure: A quantified statement.

Mission statement: Statement made by a library of its provision and development of services and products.

Objective: An individual act intended to be carried out, and a number of which are required to be carried out in order to reach a goal.

Opening hours: The average number of hours a library is open to the public from Monday to Sunday.

Outcome (= impact): The effect of library outputs on the larger environment.

Outputs: The products and services created by the library.

Performance: Performance is the degree to which a library is achieving its objectives, particularly in term of users' needs.

Performance indicator: A quantified statement used to evaluate and compare the performance of a library in achieving its objectives.

Primary user group (= capita, domain, population served, catchment population): Population to be served (primarily: members of the institution the library is meant to serve).

Quality: The totality of features and characteristics of a product or service that bear on its ability to satisfy stated or implied needs.

Random sample: Sample in which every member of the larger population has an equal chance of being chosen for the sample.

Reliability: The quality of measurement such that the same results would be achieved from repeated measures of the same phenomenon.

Remote Uses: Uses of services offered by the library on the electronic network (e.g. OPAC, CD-ROM databases, electronic publications, general information etc.) from access points outside the library or its branch libraries.

Request: A demand for library material or information by a user.

Sample: A subset of cases used to represent a larger group or population.

Sampling error: The possible difference between the estimate derived from the sample and the true value for the entire population.

User (= client, patron): Everybody who uses the services and facilities of a library.

Validity: The characteristic of indicators that accurately reflect what they are intended to measure.

French Glossary

(Academic library)
Bibliothèque d'établissement d'enseignement supérieur: Bibliothèque formant partie intégrante d'une université ou de tout autre établissement d'enseignement supérieur, organisée et administrée en vue de satisfaire les besoins d'information des étudiants, du corps enseignant et du personnel attaché à l'institution.

(Availability)
(Taux de) Disponibilité (des documents): Proportion des recherches de documents effectuées par l'usager qui sont satisfaites durant le temps de son séjour à la bibliothèque.

(Circulation)
Communication (des documents): Nombre de documents communiqués pour le prêt à domicile ou pour la consultation sur place, qu'il s'agisse de collections en accès libre, contrôlé ou différé (comprend les renouvellements).

(Cost-effectiveness)
Rapport coût-efficacité: Coût d'un service rapporté à son niveau d'efficacité.

(Degree of use)
Degré d'utilisation: Relation, pour une catégorie donnée de documents, entre la proportion des communications au public, la proportion des acquisitions annuelles et la proportion des dépenses annuelles d'acquisition par rapport aux résultats de l'ensemble du fonds.

(Document delivery)
Délai de fourniture des documents: Délai moyen entre le moment où un usager entame la procédure nécessaire pour obtenir communication d'un document et le moment où ce document est mis à sa disposition à la banque de prêt.

(Effectiveness)
Efficacité: Degré de réussite d'un service par rapport à des objectifs donnés.

(Efficiency)
Efficience: Relation entre les ressources employées et les produits ou services obtenus.

(Facilities)
Installations: Espaces et équipements offerts aux usagers d'une bibliothèque.

(Fill rate)
Taux de réponse: Proportion de recherches ou de demandes de documents ou de questions satisfaites.

(Goal)
Objectif général (programmé pour le moyen ou le long terme).

(In-house materials use)
Consultation sur place: Nombre de documents utilisés dans la bibliothèque sans enregistrement.

(Inputs)
Ressources: Moyens (matériels, humains, financiers) employés par une bibliothèque.

(Library visits)
Fréquentation: Nombre d'entrées d'usagers à la bibliothèque, incluant la participation aux activités d'animation et l'utilisation des services qui ne requièrent pas l'intervention du personnel.

(Management)
Management: Utilisation rationnelle des ressources en vue d'atteindre des objectifs déterminés.

(Market penetration)
Taux de pénétration: Proportion de la population à desservir qui utilise effectivement la bibliothèque.

(Measure)
Mesure: Détermination quantitative.

(Mission statement)
Missions fondamentales: Description formelle pour une bibliothèque des services qu'elle veut rendre et des produits qu'elle veut concevoir.

(Objective)
Objectif opérationnel: Résultat à obtenir dans le cadre d'un programme d'actions élaboré pour atteindre un objectif général.

(Opening hours)
Heures d'ouverture: Moyenne hebdomadaire des heures d'ouverture au public.

(Outcome [= impact])
Impact: Effet des produits et services réalisés par la bibliothèque sur son environnement.

(Outputs)
Produits et services (réalisés par la bibliothèque).

(Performance)
Performance: Degré jusqu'auquel une bibliothèque réalise ses objectifs, notamment en termes de satisfaction des besoins des usagers.

(Performance indicator)
Indicateur de performance: Mesure utilisée pour évaluer la réalisation des objectifs que s'est fixés une bibliothèque.

(Primary user group [= capita, domain, population served, catchment population])
Population à desservir.

(Quality)
Qualité: Ensemble des caractéristiques d'un produit ou d'un service qui déterminent son aptitude à satisfaire des besoins explicites ou implicites.

(Random sample)
Échantillonnage aléatoire: Échantillonnage tel que chaque individu d'une population donnée a le même nombre de chances d'être retenu dans l'échantillon.

(Reliability)
Fiabilité: Qualité d'une mesure qui donne les mêmes résultats toutes les fois qu'elle est appliquée dans les mêmes conditions à un même phénomène.

(Remote Uses)
Accès à distance: Utilisation des services offerts par la bibliothèque grâce à un réseau électronique (p. ex. OPAC, banques de données CD-ROM, publications électroniques, informations générales, etc.) avec possibilités d'accès de l'extérieur à la bibliothèque centrale ou à une de ces succursales.

(Request)
Demande (de document ou d'information émanant d'un usager).

(Sample)
Échantillon: Fraction d'une population destinée à représenter la population dans son ensemble.

(Sampling error)
Marge d'erreur probable: Écart probable entre l'estimation fournie par l'échantillon et la valeur réelle pour la population entière.

(User [= client, patron])
Usager: Toute personne utilisant les services ou installations d'une bibliothèque.

(Validity)
Validité: Caractère d'un indicateur qui reflète exactement ce qu'il est supposé mesurer.

German Glossary

(Academic library)
Wissenschaftliche Bibliothek: Eine Bibliothek, die integraler Bestandteil einer Hochschule oder einer anderen akademischen Einrichtung ist und darauf ausgerichtet ist, die Informations- bedürfnisse der Studenten, des Lehrkörpers und des übrigen Personals der Institution zu erfüllen.

(Availability)
Verfügbarkeit: Der Anteil der Benutzerrecherchen nach Bibliotheksmaterial, der im Verlauf eines Bibliotheksbesuchs erfolgreich abgeschlossen wird.

(Circulation)
Ausleihe: Die Zahl der ausgeliehenen Bibliotheksmaterialien, die in der Regel (jedoch nicht grundsätzlich) außerhalb der Bibliothek genutzt werden. Dies beinhaltet Erstausleihen wie Leihfristverlängerungen aus dem Freihandbestand wie aus geschlossenen Magazinen.

(Cost-effectiveness)
Kostenwirksamkeit: Die Kosten für das Erreichen eines bestimmten Grades an Effektivität.

(Degree of use)
Nutzungsgrad: Das Verhältnis zwischen dem Anteil eines Faches an der Ausleihe, dem jährlichen Zugang in diesem Fach und den für das Fach ausgegebenen Mitteln.

(Document delivery)
Bereitstellungszeit für Dokumente: Die durchschnittliche Zeitspanne zwischen dem Moment, an dem ein Benutzer mit den für einen Ausleihvorgang notwendigen Arbeitsschritten beginnt, und dem Zeitpunkt, an dem das gewünschte Dokument für ihn am Ausleihschalter bereitliegt.

(Effectiveness)
Effektivität: Der Grad, zu dem die Bibliothek ihre Augaben und Ziele erfüllt.

(Efficiency)
Effizienz: Verhältnis zwischen den eingebrachten Ressourcen und der resultierenden Leistung.

(Facilities)
Ausstattung: Räumlichkeiten und Einrichtungen, die dem Bibliotheksbenutzer zur Verfügung stehen.

(Fill rate)
Erfolgsquote: Anteil der Recherchen, Bestellungen oder Anfragen, die erfolgreich abge- schlossen oder beantwortet werden.

(Goal)
Ziel: Langfristig anvisierte Zielvorstellung, die es zu verwirklichen gilt.

(In-house materials use)
Präsenzbenutzung: Die Zahl der in der Bibliothek benutzten, aber nicht ausgeliehenen Materialien.

(Inputs)
Ressourcen: Die von der Bibliothek eingebrachten Ressourcen.

(Library visits)
Bibliotheksbesuche: Die Zahl der Benutzerbesuche, wobei jedes Betreten der Bibliothek als Besuch gezählt wird. Dazu gehören die Teilnahme an Veranstaltungen aller Art ebenso wie solche Besuche, bei denen keine Dienstleistung seitens des Personals erforderlich wird.

(Management)
Unternehmensführung: Die Nutzung von materiellen wie personellen Ressourcen, um festgelegte Ziele zu erreichen.

(Market penetration)
Marktdurchdringung: Der Anteil an der Gesamtheit der potentiellen Benutzerschaft einer Bibliothek, der tatsächlich die Dienste der Bibliothek in Anspruch nimmt.

(Measure)
Meßgröße: Eine quantitative Aussage.

(Mission statement)
Auftragsformulierung: Formale Beschreibung für eine Bibliothek, welche Dienstleistungen und Produkte sie bereitstellen und entwickeln will.

(Objective)
Nahziel: Einzelne Aufgaben, deren Verwirklichung zusammen das Erreichen eines langfristigen Zieles gewährleistet.

(Opening hours)
Öffnungszeiten: Die Anzahl der Wochenstunden (einschließlich Wochenende), die eine Bibliothek für die Öffentlichkeit zugänglich ist.

(Outcome [= impact])
Resultat (= Wirksamkeit): Die Auswirkung der Bibliotheksleistung auf das sozio-ökonomische Umfeld.

(Outputs)
Erträge: Die von der Bibliothek erbrachten Produkte und Dienstleistungen.

(Performance)
Leistung: Der Grad, zu dem die Bibliothek ihre Ziele erreicht, insbesondere in Hinsicht auf die Benutzerbedürfnisse.

(Performance indicator)
Leistungsindikator: Eine quantifizierte Aussage, die Leistung einer Bibliothek hinsichtlich des Erreichens ihrer Ziele zu bewerten und zu vergleichen.

(Primary user group)
Primäre Nutzergruppe: Gesamtheit der von einer Bibliothek zu versorgenden Benutzerschaft (in erster Linie: Angehörige der Institution, für die die Bibliothek Dienstleistungen zu erbringen hat).

(Quality)
Qualität: Die Gesamtheit von Merkmalen und Eigenschaften eines Produkts oder einer Dienstleistung, die sich auf das Vermögen auswirken, explizite und implizite Bedürfnisse zu befriedigen.

(Random sample)
Zufallsstichprobe: Eine Stichprobe, bei der jede Einheit einer Grundgesamtheit die gleiche Chance hat, in der Auswahl vertreten zu sein.

(Reliability)
Zuverlässigkeit: Die Eigenschaft einer Meßgröße, wonach bei der Analyse desselben Sachverhalts unter vergleichbaren Bedingungen bei wiederholten Messungen dasselbe Ergebnis erzielt wird.

(Remote Uses)
Fernnutzung: Die Nutzungen von Dienstleistungen, die von der Bibliothek über ein elektronisches Netzwerk angeboten werden (z.B. OPAC, CD-ROM Datenbanken, elektronische Publikationen, allgemeine Informationen usw.) mit Zugangsmöglichkeiten von außerhalb der Bibliothek oder ihrer Zweigbibliotheken.

(Request)
Anfrage: Nachfrage nach Bibliotheksmaterial oder Information durch einen Benutzer.

(Sample)
Stichprobe: Eine Auswahl von Einheiten, die eine größere Gruppe oder Grundgesamtheit repräsentieren.

(Sampling error)
Stichprobenfehler: Die mögliche Abweichung zwischen der aus einer Auswahl abgeleiteten Schätzung und dem eigentlichen Wert für die Grundgesamtheit.

(User [= client, patron])
Benutzer: Jeder, der die Dienstleistungen und Einrichtungen der Bibliothek benutzt.

(Validity)
Stichhaltigkeit: Die Eigenschaft eines Indikators, genau das wiederzugeben, was er zu messen beabsichtigt.

Russian Glossary

(Academic library)
Vuzovskaja biblioteka: Biblioteka, javljajuščajasja neot"emlemoj sostavnoj čast'ju kolledža, universiteta ili drugogo vysšego učebnogo zavedenija, prednaznačennaja dlja udovletvorenija informacionnych potrebnostej studentov, professorsko-prepodavatel'skogo sostava i drugich sotrudnikov dannogo učebnogo zavedenija.

(Availability)
Dostupnost': Stepen' udovletvorenija potrebnostej pol'zovatelja v bibliotečnych materialach vo vremja poseščenija biblioteki.

(Circulation)
Knigovydača: Količestvo dokumentov. vydannych dlja pol'zovanija, kak pravilo (no ne tol'ko), za predelami biblioteki. Vključaet pervičnye zakazy i zakazy na prodlenie sroka pol'zovanija bibliotečnymi materialami kak iz osnovnogo, tak i iz rezervnogo fonda.

(Cost-effectiveness)
Rentabel'nost': Zatraty na dostiženie opredelennogo urovnja éffektivnosti.

(Degree of use)
Stepen' popol'zovanija: Sootnošenie meždu pokazateljami knigovydači i ežegodnych postuplenij bibliotečnych materialov po opredelennoj tematike i dolej bjudžetnych raschodov na ich priobretenie.

(Document delivery)
Dostavka dokumentov: Srednij promežutok vremeni ot momenta načala operacij, svjazannych s zakazom dokumenta, do momenta ego postuplenija na kafedru vydači.

(Effectiveness)
Éffektivnost': Stepen' dostiženija bibliotekoj postavlennych celej i zadač.

(Efficiency)
Ékonomičeskaja éffektivnost': Sootnošenie meždu zatračennymi resursami i konečnym produktom.

(Facilities)
Zdanija i oborudovanie: Ploščadi i oborudovanie, predostavljaemye v rasporjaženie pol'zovatelej biblioteki.

(Fill rate)
Pokazatel' vypolnenija: Sootnošenie vypolnennych zaprosov s ich obščim čislom.

(Goal)
Cel': Ustojčivoe položenie del, kotoroe dolžno byt' dostignuto i obespečeno na prodolžitel'nyj period.

126

(In-house materials use)
Ispol'zovanie materialov vnutri biblioteki: Količestvo dokumentov, ispol'zuemych v biblioteke, no ne vydavaemych po abonementu.

(Inputs)
Proizvodstvennye zatraty: Resursy, ispol'zuemye bibliotekoj.

(Library visits)
Količestvo poseščenij: Količestvo čitatelej, prichodjaščich v biblioteku, vključaja poseščajuščich sobranija i učastvujuščich v drugich vidach bibliotečnoj dejatel'nosti, a takže tech, kto ne trebuet obsluživanija personalom biblioteki.

(Management)
Upravlenie: Ispol'zovanie material'nych i čelovečeskich resursov dlja dostiženija postavlennych celej.

(Market penetration)
Ochvat pol'zovatelej: Sootnošenie čisla faktičeskich i potencial'nych pol'zovatelej biblioteki.

(Measure)
Pokazatel': Količestvennoe vyraženie kakoj-libo veličiny.

(Mission statement)
Programmnyj dokument: Dokument, soderžaščij opisanie i načertanie dal'nejšego razvitija služb i produktov, predostavlennych bibliotekoj.

(Objective)
Zadača: Otdel'noe dejstvie, kotoroe dolžno byt' osuščestvleno v rjadu drugich dejstvij, neobchodimych dlja dostiženija postavlennoj celi.

(Opening hours)
Časy raboty: Srednee količestvo časov, v tečenie kotorych biblioteka otkryta dlja čitatelej s ponedel'nika do voskresen'ja.

(Outcome [= impact])
Vychod (= vozdejstvie): Vlijanie rezul'tatov dejatel'nosti biblioteki na vnešnee okruženie.

(Outputs)
Konečnyj produkt: Sozdavaemye bibliotekoj produkty i okazyvaemye eju uslugi.

(Performance)
Èffektivnost' raboty: Stepen' dostiženija bibliotekoj postavlennych celej, prežde vsego s točki zrenija udovletvorenija potrebnostej čitatelej.

(Performance indicator)
Pokazatel' èffektivnosti: Količestvennoe vyraženie, ispol'zuemoe dlja ocenki dejatel'nosti biblioteki s točki zrenija dostiženija postavlennych celej.

127

Glossaries

(**Primary user group** [= **capita, domain, population served, catchment population**])
Osnovnaja gruppa pol'zovatelej (= **obsluživaemaja territorija, obsluživaemoe naselenie**):
Naselenie, obsluživaemoe bibliotekoj (v pervuju očered', sotrudniki učreždenija,
oblsuživaemogo dannoj bibliotekoj).

(**Quality**)
Kačestvo: Sovokupnost' priznakov i svojstv produkta ili uslugi, otražajuščich stepen'
sootvetstvija dannogo produkta ili uslugi točno opredelennym ili predpolagaemym
trebovanijam.

(**Random sample**)
Slučajnaja vyborka: Vyborka, popast' v kotoruju s odinakovoj verojatnost'ju možet ljuboj
čelovek.

(**Reliability**)
Nadežnost': Takoe kačestvo izmerenija, kotoroe obespečivaet polučenie odinakovych rezul'tatov
pri povtornych izmerenijach.

(**Remote Uses**)
Obsluživanie udalennych pol'zovatelej: Vidy pol'zovanija bibliotekoj, kotorye ne trebujut
prichoda v biblioteku, t.e. ispol'zovanie služb, predlagaemych élektronnoj set'ju (napr. OPAC,
bazy dannych na CD-ROM, élektronnye publikacii, obščie informacii) s terminalov,
nachodjaščichsja za predelami biblioteki i ee filialov.

(**Request**)
Zapros (= **trebovanie**): Zajavka pol'zovatelja na polučenie bibliotečnogo materiala ili
informacii.

(**Sample**)
Vyborka: Gruppa ljudej, predstavljajuščich otnositel'no širokij krug naselenija (pri provedenii
issledovanija).

(**Sampling error**)
Ošibka vyborki: Vozmožnaja raznica meždu rassčitannoj schemoj i general'noj sovokupnost'ju.

(**User** [= **client, patron**])
Pol'zovatel' (= **potrebitel', čitatel'**): Ljuboe lico, pol'zujuščeesja uslugami biblioteki, ee
zdanijami i oborudovaniem.

(**Validity**)
Validnost': Charakteristika pokazatelej, točno otražajuščich to, čto oni prizvany vyražat'.

Spanish Glossary

(Academic library)
Biblioteca universitaria: Biblioteca que es parte integrante de una universidad u otra institución académica de educación postsecundaria, organizada y administrada para satisfacer les necesidades de información de los estudiantes, profesores y personal de la institución.

(Availability)
Disponibilidad: Proporción de búsquedas de materiales de la biblioteca que el usuario reliza satisfactoriamente durante su visita.

(Circulation)
Circulación: Número de ejemplares prestados para su uso, generalmente (aunque no siempre) fuera de la biblioteca. Incluye el préstamo inicial y las renovaciones, colección general y reservas.

(Cost-effectiveness)
Coste-eficacia: Coste de alcanzar unos determinados resultados.

(Degree of use)
Nivel de utilizacion: Relación, para una determinada materia, entre los porcentajes de circulación, del volumen anual de adquisiciones y del gasto anual en dicha materia.

(Document delivery)
Suministro de documentos: Tiempo medio entre el momento en que un usuario comienza los procedimientos de préstamo y el momento en que el ejemplar está disponible para ser retirado en préstamo.

(Effectiveness)
Eficacia: Grado alcanzado por la biblioteca en el cumplimiento de sus metas y objetivos.

(Efficiency)
Efectividad: Relación entre los recursos y los resultados.

(Facilities)
Instalaciones: Espacio y equipamiento disponibles para los usuarios de la biblioteca.

(Fill rate)
Tasa alcanzada: Proporción de búsquedas y peticiones o preguntas satisfechas.

(Goal)
Meta: Línea fundamental de actuación que se formula con una perspectiva de permanencia.

(In-house materials use)
Consulta en sala: Uso de documentos en la biblioteca, no servidos en préstamo.

(Inputs)
Recursos: Medios materiales y humanos con que cuenta la biblioteca.

(Library visits)
Visitas a la biblioteca: Entradas que los usuarios efectúan a la biblioteca, incluyendo los que asisten a actividades, reuniones y otros fines que no requieren servicios del personal.

(Management)
Gestión/administración: Utilización de los recursos humanos y materiales para alcanzar las metas propuestas.

(Market penetratión)
Penetracion de mercado: Proporción de usuarios potenciales de la biblioteca que la utilizan de hecho.

(Measure)
Medida: Proposición cuantificada.

(Mission statement)
Misión: Enunciado hecho por una biblioteca acerca de los servicios y productos que desea preparer y desarrollar.

(Objective)
Objetivo: Acción específica que se pretende llevar a cabo, siendo necesarias varias de ellas para alcanzar una meta.

(Opening hours)
Horas de apertura: Número de horas que una biblioteca está abierta al público, de lunes a domingo.

(Outcome [= impact])
Resultado (= impacto): Efecto de la actividad de la biblioteca en su área de influencia.

(Outputs)
Actividad: Productos y servicios ofrecidos por la bilioteca.

(Performance)
Rendimiento: Grado de cumplimiento de los objetivos de una biblioteca, particularmente definido en términos de necesidades de los usuarios.

(Performance indicator)
Indicador de rendimiento: Proposición cuantificada que se utiliza para evaluar y comparar el grado de cumplimiento de los objetivos de una biblioteca.

(Primary user group)
Grupo principal de usuarios: Población a la que se sirve (principalmente los miembros de la institución a la que la biblioteca atiende).

(Quality)
Calidad: Conjunto de características de un producto o servicio relacionadas con su capacidad de satisfacer necesidades definidas o implícitas.

(Random sample)
Muestra estadística: Conjunto de individuos de una población cuya probabilidad de ser escogidos es la misma.

(Reliability)
Fiabilidad: Cualidad de una medición, por la que midiendo repetidamente un fenómeno se obtienen los mismos resultados.

(Remote Uses)
Usos remotos: Usos de los servicios ofrecidos por la biblioteca en la red electrónica (p.ej. OPAC, bancos de datos CD-ROM, publicaciones electrónicas, informaciones generales, etc.) con acceso desde fuera de la biblioteca o de sus bibliotecas sucursales.

(Request)
Solicitud: Petición de matriales o información que el usario realiza a la biblioteca.

(Sample)
Muestra: Subconjunto de casos utilizados para representar a un grupo o población mayor.

(Sampling error)
Error de muestreo: Posible diferencia entre la estimación resultado de la muestra y el valor real para el conjunto de la población.

(User [= client, patron])
Usuario (= lector): Toda persona que utiliza las instalaciones y servicios de la biblioteca.

(Validity)
Validez: Característica de indicadores que reflejan de manera ajustada lo que se proponen medir.

Selected

Bibliography

Selected Bibliography

This bibliography is meant to cover the main topics in the field of evaluation and measurement of academic library services within the last 20 years. It includes, however, some pre-1976 titles as well as some articles on public libraries which we thought were of particular importance.

Handbooks and Guidelines

THE EFFECTIVE ACADEMIC LIBRARY: A Framework for Evaluating the Performance of UK Academic Libraries / A Consultative Report to the HEFCE, SHEFC, HEFCW and DENI by the Joint Funding Councils' Ad Hoc Group on Performance Indicators for Libraries. London, 1995

ISO / CD 11620.2 : 1995. Information and Documentation - Library Performance Indicators

KEYS TO SUCCESS: Performance Indicators for Public Libraries / A Manual of Performance Measures and Indicators Developed by King Research Ltd. - London: HMSO, 1990. - (Library Information Series ; 18)

LIBRARY PERFORMANCE INDICATORS: CLIENT SATISFACTION; DOCUMENT DELIVERY; AVAILABILITY OF SOUGHT MATERIALS / Council of Australian University Librarians. - Richmond: CAVAL Ltd, 1995 (three floppy disks)

MOORE, NICK: Measuring the Performance of Public Libraries / Prepared by Nick Moore for the General Information Programme and UNISIST. - Paris: UNESCO, 1989

OUTPUT MEASURES FOR PUBLIC LIBRARIES: A Manual of Standardized Procedures / Prepared for the Public Library Development Project by Nancy A. VanHouse, Mary Jo Lynch, Charles R. McClure, Douglas L. Zweizig, Eleanor Jo Rodger. - 2nd ed. - Chicago: American Library Association, 1987

PERFORMANCE INDICATORS FOR UNIVERSITY LIBRARIES: A Practical Guide / Standing Committee of National and University Libraries : Advisory Committee on Performance Indicators . - London: Sconul, 1992.

SUMSION, JOHN: Practical Performance Indicators. - 1992: Documenting the Citizens'Charter Consultation for U.K. Public Libraries with Examples of PIs and Surveys in Use. - Loughborough: Library and Information Statistics Unit, 1993. - (LISU Occasional Paper ; No. 5)

SUMSION, JOHN; SUZANNE WARD: Performance Indicators and Library Management Models. - Office of the European Communities, 1995 (EUR 16448EN)

VANHOUSE, NANCY A.; BETH T. WEIL ; CHARLES R. MCCLURE: Measuring Academic Library Performance: A Practical Approach. - Chicago: American Libr. Assoc., 1990

Bibliography

AANONSON, JOHN: A Comparison of Keyword Subject Searching on Six British University Opacs
In: Online Review. - 11 (1987), pp. 303 - 313

ABBOTT, CHRISTINE: Performance Indicators in a Quality Context
In: Law Librarian. - 25 (1994), pp. 205 - 208

ABBOTT, CHRISTINE: Performance Measurement in Library and Information Services. - London: Aslib, 1994

135

ABBOTT, CHRISTINE: What Does Good Look Like?: The Adoption of Performance Indicators at Aston University Library and Information Services
In: British Journal of Academic Librarianship. - 5 (1990), pp. 79 - 94

ACADEMIC LIBRARY MANAGEMENT: Edited Papers of a British Council Sponsored Course, 15 - 27 January 1989, Birmingham / Ed. by Maurice B. Line. - London: Library Association, 1990

AGUILAR, W.: The Application of Relative Use and Interlibrary Demand in Collection Development
In: Collection Development. - 8 (1986), pp. 15 - 24

ALLAN, ANN; KATHY J. REYNOLDS: Performance Problems: A Model for Analysis and Resolution
In: Journal of Academic Librarianship. - 9 (1983), pp. 83 - 88

ALLDREDGE, NOREEN S.: The Preparation of Guidelines for Evaluating Performance of Vendors for In-print Monographs
In: Issues in Acquisitions: Programms and Evaluation / Ed. by Sul H. Lee. - Ann Arbor, Michigan, 1984, pp. 1 - 10

ALLRED, JOHN: The Evaluation of Academic Library Services
In: Management Issues in Academic Libraries: Proceedings of the Joint Annual Study Conference, Chester, 1-4 April 1985. - London, 1986, pp. 22 - 31

ALSBURY, DONNA: Vendor Performance Evaluation as a Model for Evaluating Acquisitions
In: Acquisitions Librarian. - 6 (1991), pp. 93 - 103

ALTMAN, E.: A Data Gathering and Instructional Manual for Performance Measures in Public Libraries. - Chicago: Celadon Press, 1976

ALTMAN, ELLEN: Reflections on Performance Measures Fifteen Years Later
In: Library Performance, Accountability and Responsiveness: Essays in Honor of Ernest R. DeProspo / Ed. by Charles C.Curran and F. William Summers. - Norwood, N. J.: Ablex (1990), pp. 1 - 16

AMERICAN LIBRARY ASSOCIATION.Collection Management and Development Committee and the Acquisitions Committee, Resource Section, Resources and Technical Services Division: Guide to Performance Evaluation of Library Materials Vendors. - Chicago: American Library Association, 1988. - (Acquisitions guidelines ; 5)

ANDERSON, JUDY: Have Users Changed Their Style? A Survey of CD-ROM vs. OPAC Product Usage
In: RQ. - 34 (1995), pp. 362 - 368

ANDERSON, WILLIAM: Evolution of Library and Information Services for Special Groups: The Role of Performance Review and the Use
In: INSPEL. - 25 (1991), pp. 37 - 46

ANKENY, MELVON L.: Evaluating End-user Services: Success or Satisfaction?
In: Journal of Academic Librarianship. - 16 (1991), pp. 352 - 356

AREN, LISA J.; SUSAN J. WEBRECK: Costing Library Operations - A Bibliography
In: Collection Building. - 8 (1987), pp. 23 - 28

ARTHUR, ANTONY J.: Collection Management: An Australian Project
In: Australian Academic and Research Libraries. - 17 (1986), pp. 29 - 38

ASH, LEE: Old Dog; No Tricks: Perceptions of the Qualitative Analysis of Book Collections
In: Library Trends. - 33 (1985), pp. 385 - 395

ÅSLUND, HENRIK: Öppettider/Service: Rapport från biblioteksundersökningen vid Stockholms universitetsbibliotek den 14-20 november 1994. - Stockholm: Universitetsbibliotek, 1994

AUCKLAND, MARY: Performance Measurement in Academic Libraries: Report on a Workshop held by the Section of University Libraries and other General Research Libraries at the 55th IFLA Council and General Conference in Paris, August 1989
In: Outlook on Research Libraries. - 11 (1989), pp. 3 - 6

AXFORD, H. WILLIAM: Performance Measurement Revisited
In: College and Research Libraries. - 34 (1973), pp. 249 - 257

BACH, HARRY: Scientific Literature Use: A Survey
In: Special Libraries. - 48 (1957), p. 466

BAILEY, BILL: The "55 Percent Rule" Revisited
In: Journal of Academic Librarianship. - 13 (1987), pp. 280 - 281

BAKER, SHARON L.: Problem Solving through Experimental Research: The Need for Better Controls
In: Library Trends. - 38 (1989), pp. 204 - 214

BARBUTO, DOMENICA M.; ELENA E. CEVALLOS: The Delivery of Reference Services in a CD-ROM LAN Environment: A Case Study
In: RQ. - 34 (1994), pp. 60 - 76

BARKER, JOSEPH W.: Random Vendor Assignment in Vendor Performance Evaluation
In: Library Acquisitions: Practice and Theory. - 10 (1986), pp. 265 - 280

BARR, AIALA; HERBERT S. SICHEL: A Bivariate Model to Predict Library Circulation
In: Journal of the American Society for Information Science. - 42 (1991), pp. 546 - 553

BARREAU, DEBORAH K.: Using Performance Measures to Implement an Online Catalog
In: Library Resources and Technical Services. - 32 (1992), pp. 312 - 322

BAUMANN, SUSAN: An Application of Davis' "Model for a Vendor Study"
In: Library Acquisitions: Practice and Theory. - 8 (1984), pp. 83 - 90

BAUMANN, SUSAN: An Extended Application of Davis' "Model for a Vendor Study"
In: Library Acquisitions: Practice and Theory. - 9 (1985), pp. 317 - 329

BAUMOL, W. J.; M. MARCUS: Economics of Academic Libraries. - Washington, D.C.: American Council of Education, 1973

BAWDEN, DAVID: User-oriented Evaluation of Information Systems and Services. - Aldershot: Gower, 1990. - 209p.

BECK, WILLIAM L.; MARSHAL NOLF: The Process and Value of Self-study in a Medium-sized University Library
In: College and Research Libraries. - 53 (1992), pp. 150 - 162

BEHESTI, JAMSHID; JEAN TAGUE: Morse's Markov Model of Book Use Revisited
In: Journal of the American Society for Information Science. - 35 (1984), pp. 259 - 267

BENHAM, F.; R. R. POWELL: Success in Answering Reference Questions: Two Studies. - Metuchen, N.J.: Scarecrow Press, 1987

BENNION, B. C.; S. KARSCHAMROON: Multivariate Regression Models for Estimating Journal Usefulness in Physics
In: Journal of Documentation. - 40 (1984), pp. 217 - 227

BERDIE, DOUG R.; JOHN F. ANDERSON; MARSHA A. NIEBUHR: Questionnaires: Design and Use. - 2nd ed. - Metuchen, N.J.: Scarecrow Press, 1986

BERGER, MARILYN; JANE DEVINE: Serials Evaluation: An Innovative Approach
In: Special Libraries. - 81 (1990), pp. 183 - 188

BERKNER, DIMITY S.: Communication between Vendors and Librarians: The Bookseller's Point of View
In: Library Acquisitions: Practice and Theory. - 3 (1979), pp. 85 - 90

BERTLAND, LINDA H.: Circulation Analysis as a Tool for Collection Development
In: School Library Media Quarterly. - 19 (1991), pp. 90 - 97

BETRIEBSVERGLEICH AN ÖFFENTLICHEN BIBLIOTHEKEN: ein Zwischenbericht aus dem Projekt der Bertelsmann Stiftung / (verantw.: Bettina Windau). - Gütersloh: Verl. Bertelsmann Stiftung, 1994

BETTS, D. A.; R. HARGRAVE: How Many Books? - Bradford: MCB Publications, 1982

BIRBECK, VAUGHAN P.; KENNETH A. WHITTAKER: Room for Improvement: An Unobtrusive Testing of British Public Library Reference Service
In: Public Library Journal. - 2 (1987), pp. 55 - 60

BJARNO, HELLE: Cost Finding and Performance Measures in ILL Management
In: Interlending and Document Supply. - 22 (1994), pp. 8 - 11

BLAGDEN, JOHN; J. HARRINGTON: How Good Is Your Library?: A Review of Approaches to the Evaluation of Library and Information Services. - London: ASLIB, 1990

BLAGDEN, JOHN: Performance Assessment - The How and the What
In: Do We Really Need Libraries?: Proceedings of the First Joint Library Association Cranfield Institute of Technology Conference on Performance Assessment / Ed. by John Blagden. -Cranfield, 1983, pp. 1 - 8

BLAGDEN, JOHN: Some Thoughts on Use and Users
In: IATUL Quarterly. - 2 (1988), pp. 125 - 134

BLAND, R. N.: The College Textbook as a Tool for Collection Evaluation, Analysis, and Retrospective Collection Development
In: Library Acquisitions: Practice and Theory. - 4 (1980), pp. 193 - 197

BLOOR, IAN: "Keys to Success": A User's Guide
In: Public Library Journal. - 5 (1990), pp. 133 - 144

BLOOR, IAN: Performance Indicators and Decision Support Systems for Libraries: A Practical Application of "Keys to Success". - London: British Library, 1991 . - (British Library Research Paper ; 93)

BOEKHORST, PETER TE: Leistungsmessung in wissenschaftlichen Bibliotheken: Neue Initiativen
In: Nachrichten für Dokumentation. - 46 (1995), pp. 121 - 126

BOEKHORST, PETER TE: Measuring Quality: The IFLA Guidelines for Performance Measurement in Academic Libraries
In: IFLA Journal. - 21 (1995), pp. 278 - 281

BOEKHORST, PETER TE: Methoden der Leistungsmessung in Bibliotheken: die Durchführung einer Verfügbarkeitsstudie an der UB Münster
In: Bibliothek. Forschung und Praxis. - 16 (1992), pp. 153 - 161

BOEKHORST, PETER TE; ROSWITHA POLL: Beschaffungsgeschwindigkeit: Leistungsmessung auf dem Gebiet der Erwerbung
In: Bibliotheken, Service für die Zukunft / 5. Dt. Bibliothekskongreß, 83. Deutscher Bibliothekartag in Leipzig 1993. Hartwig Lohse (Ed.). - Frankfurt/Main: Klostermann, 1994. - (Zeitschrift für Bibliothekswesen und Bibliographie: Sonderheft ; 58), pp. 123 - 137

BOMMER, M. R.: The Development of a Management System for Effective Decision Making and Planning in a University Library. - Philadelphia: University of Pennsylvania, Wharton School of Finance and Commerce, 1973

BONN, GEORGE S.: Evaluation of the Collection
In: Library Trends. - 22 (1973), pp. 265 - 304

BOOKSTEIN, ABRAHAM; A. LINDSAY: Questionnaire Ambiguity: A Rasch Scaling Model Analysis
In: Library Trends. - 38 (1989), pp. 215 - 236

BOOKSTEIN, ABRAHAM: Questionnaire Research in a Library Setting
In: Journal of Academic Librarianship. - 11 (1985), pp. 24 - 28

BOOKSTEIN, ABRAHAM: Sources of Error in Library Questionnaires
In: Library Research. - 4 (1982), pp. 85 - 94

BORKOWSKI, C.; M. J. MACLEOD: The Implications of Some Recent Studies of Library Use
In: Scholarly Publishing. - 11 (1979), pp. 3 - 24

BOSMAN, F. E.; M. A. H. ONGERING; H. P. A. SMIT: Observeren en registreren: Evaluatieonderzoek naar OPC3
In: Open. - 25 (1993), pp. 352 - 356

BOURNE, C. P.; J. ROBINSON: SDI Citation Checking as a Measure of the Performance of Library Document Delivery Systems. - Berkeley, Cal.: University of California at Berkeley, Institute of Library Research, 1973

BRACKEN, JAMES K.; JOHN C. CALHOUN: Profiling Vendor Performance
In: Library Resources and Technical Services. - 28 (1984), pp. 120 - 128

BRAUNSTEIN, Y. M.: Costs and Benefits of Library Information: The User Point of View
In: Library Trends. - 28 (1979), pp. 79 - 87

BRINDLEY, LYNNE: Performance Measurement: Can You Manage without It? Summing up
In: British Journal of Academic Librarianship. - 4 (1989), pp. 121 - 126

BRINDLEY, LYNNE J.: Library Development Plans: A Case Study; Aston University Library and Information Services
In: British Journal of Academic Librarianship. - 5 (1990), pp. 155 - 158

BRITTEN, WILLIAM A.; JUDITH D. WEBSTER: Comparing Characteristics of Highly Circulated Titles for Demand-driven Collection Development
In: College and Research Libraries. - 53 (1992), pp. 239 - 248

BROADBENT, ELAINE: A Study of the Use of the Subject Catalog, Marriott Library, University of Utah
In: Cataloging and Classification Quarterly. - 4 (1984), pp. 75 - 83

BROADUS, ROBERT N.: Use Studies of Library Collections
In: Library Resources and Technical Services. - 24 (1980), pp. 317 - 324

BROOKES, B. C.: Obsolescence of Special Library Periodicals: Sampling Errors and Utility Contours
In: Journal of the American Society for Information Science. - 21 (1970), pp. 320 - 329

BROOKES, B. C.: The Growth, Utility, and Obsolescence of Scientific Periodical Literature
In: Journal of Documentation. - 26 (1970), pp. 283 - 294

BROPHY, PETER: Management Information and Decision Support Systems in Libraries. - Aldershot: Gower, 1986

BROPHY, PETER: The Mission of the Academic Library
In: British Journal of Academic Librarianship. - 6 (1991), pp. 135 - 147

BROPHY, PETER: Performance Measurement in Academic Libraries: A Polytechnic Perspective
In: British Journal of Academic Librarianship. - 4 (1989), pp. 99 - 110

BROPHY, PETER AND KATE COULLING: Quality Management for Information and Library Managers. - Aldershot:
Gower, 1996

BROUDE, J.: Journal Selection in an Academic Environment: A Comparison of Faculty and Librarian Choices
In: Serials Librarian. - 3 (1978), pp. 147 - 166

BROWN, BARRY: Triage Assessment and Management Measures for Access Services
In: Collection Management. - 17 (1992), pp. 217 - 235

BROWN, JANET DAGENAIS: Using Quality Concepts to Improve Reference Services
In: College and Research Libraries. - 55 (1994), pp. 211 - 219

BROWN, L.C.B.: Vendor Evaluation
In: Collection Management. - 19 (1995), pp. 47 - 56

BROWNSON, CHARLES W.: A Method for Evaluating Vendor Performance
In: Acquisitions Librarian. - 5 (1991), pp. 37 - 51

BRYANT, PHILIP: Performance Measures for National Bibliographic Services
In: Alexandria. - 1 (1989), pp. 27 - 35

BUCH, HARALD; PETER TE BOEKHORST: Benutzerzufriedenheit: Umfrage in der Universität- und Landesbibliothek
Münster
In: Bibliotheksdienst. - 30 (1996), to be published

BUCKLAND, MICHAEL K.: Book Availability and the Library User. - New York: Pergamon, 1975

BUCKLAND, MICHAEL K.; A. HINDLE: Loan Policies, Duplication and Availability
In: Planning Library Services: Proceedings of a Research Seminar Held at the University of Lancaster 9-11 July
1969 / Ed. by A. G. Mackenzie and I. M. Stuart. - Lancaster, 1969, pp. 1 - 16

BUCKLAND, MICHAEL K.: Methodological Problems in Assessing the Overlap Between Bibliographic Files and
Library Holdings
In: Information Processing and Management. - 11 (1975), pp. 89 - 105

BUCKLAND, MICHAEL K.: An Operations Research Study of a Variable Loan and Duplication Policy at the
University of Lancaster
In: Library Quarterly. - 42 (1972), pp. 97 - 106

BUCKLAND, MICHAEL K.: Systems Analysis of a University Library. - Lancaster: University of Lancaster Library,
1970

BULICK, STEPHEN; K. LEON MONTGOMERY; JOHN FETTERMAN; ALLEN KENT: Use of Library Materials in Terms of Age
In: Journal of the American Society for Information Science. - 27 (1976), pp. 175 -178

BUNGE, C. A.: Professional Education and Reference Efficiency. Springfield, Ill.: Illinois State Library, 1967

BURGERS, GERDA: Vertrouwen in de bibliotheek als informatiebron?: kwaliteit van inlichtingenwerk
In: Bibliotheek en Samenleving. - 18 (1990), pp. 89 - 90

BURNS, R. W.: Library Performance Measures as Seen in the Descriptive Statistics Generated by a Computer Managed Circulation System. - s.l., 1975

BURR, R. L.: Evaluating Library Collections: A Case Study
In: Journal of Academic Librarianship. - 5 (1979), pp. 256 - 260

BURTON, PAUL F.; ANDREW M. HAWKINS: Accuracy of Information Provision: The Need for Client-centred Service
In: Journal of Librarianship. - 22 (1990), pp. 201 - 215

BURTON, PETER A.: Attitudes to an Online Public Access Catalogue in an Academic Library
In: Library Management. - 14 (1993), pp. 13 - 15

BUSMIENE, STASE: Report about the Investigation "General Library Use and Facilities" and Interpretation of Its Results
In: Library Management Development Project. 3rd Report - Preliminary. - Stockholm: Universitetsbibliotek, 1995, pp. 1 - 18

BUZZARD, M. L.; D. E. NEW: An Investigation of Collection Support for Doctoral Research
In: College and Research Libraries. - 44 (1983), pp. 469 - 475

BYRD, G. D.: Collection Development Using Interlibrary Loan Borrowing and Acquisitions Statistics
In: Bulletin of the Medical Library Association. - 70 (1982), pp. 1 - 9

CALVERT, PHILIP J.: Library Effectiveness: The Search for a Social Context
In: Journal of Librarianship and Information Sciences. - 26 (1994), pp. 15 - 21

CALVERT, PHILIP J.; ROWENA CULLEN: The New Zealand Public Libraries Effectiveness Study and the New Zealand University Libraries Effectiveness Study
In: Australian Academic and Research Libraries. - 26 (1995), pp. 97 - 106

CAMERON-MILLER, BRENDA: Planning for Success: Document Workflow in the Circulation Department
In: Collection Management. - 17 (1992), pp. 167-175

CARBONE, PIERRE: The Committee Draft of International Standard ISO CD 11620 on Library Performance Indicators
In: IFLA Journal. - 21 (1995), pp. 274 - 277

CARBONE, PIERRE: Survey of the Development of Library Performance Measures in France
In: INSPEL. - 27 (1993), pp. 196 - 198

CARON, COLETTE; LISE WILSON: L'Évaluation de l'Efficacité de la Bibliothèque de Collège: Une Approche Systématique
In: Documentation et Bibliothèques. - 24 (1978), pp. 137 - 140

CATALOG USE STUDY / Ed. by V. Mostecky. - Chicago, Ill.: American Library Association, 1958

CENTRE FOR INTERFIRM COMPARISONS: Inter-library Comparisons in Academic Libraries. - London: British Library, 1984. - (British Library Research and Development Reports; 5763)

CHACHA, ROSEMARY N; ANN IRVING: An Experiment in Academic Library Performance Measurement In: British Journal of Academic Librarianship. - 6 (1991), pp. 13 - 26

CHAMBERLAIN, CAROL E.: Evaluating Acquisitions Service: New Concepts and Changing Perceptions In: Acquisitions Librarian. - 6 (1991), pp. 71 - 82

CHAMBERLAIN, CAROL E.: Evaluating Library Acquisitions Service In: Encyclopedia of Library and Information Science / Ed. Allen Kent. - Vol. 56, Suppl. 19. - New York: Dekker, 1995, pp. 118 - 126

CHANG, AMY: Quality Access Services: Maximizing and Managing In: Collection Management. - 17 (1992), pp. 63 - 75

CHEN, C. C.: The Use Patterns of Physics Journals in a Large Academic Research Library In: Journal of the American Society for Information Science. - 23 (1972), pp. 254 - 270

CHEWEH, STEVEN S.: User Criteria for Evaluation of Library Service In: Journal of Library Administration. - 2 (1981), pp. 35 - 46

CHILDERS, THOMAS; NANCY A. VANHOUSE: Dimensions of Public Library Effectiveness In: Library and Information Science Research. - 11 (1989), pp. 273 - 301

CHILDERS, THOMAS: Do Library Systems Make a Difference? In: Library Performance, Accountability and Responsiveness: Essays in Honor of Ernest R. DeProspo / Ed. by Charles C. Curran and F. William Summers. - Norwood, 1990, pp. 42 - 52

CHILDERS, THOMAS: The Effectiveness of Information Service in Public Libraries: Suffolk County In: Library Journal. - 15 (1980), pp. 924 - 928

CHILDERS, THOMAS: Evaluative Research in the Library and Information Field In: Library Trends. - 38 (1989), pp. 250 - 267

CHILDERS, THOMAS: Managing the Quality of Reference/Information Service In: Library Quarterly. - 42 (1972), pp. 212 - 217

CHILDERS, THOMAS; NANCY A. VANHOUSE:: The Public Library Effectiveness Study: Final Report. - Washington, D. C.: Department of Education, 1989

CHILDERS, THOMAS: The Quality of Reference: Still Moot after 20 Years In: Journal of Academic Librarianship.- 13 (1987), pp. 73 - 74

CHRISTENSEN, JOHN O.; LARRY D. BENSON; H. JULENE BUTLER; BLAINE H. HALL; DON H. HOWARD: An Evaluation of Reference Desk Service In: College and Research Libraries. - 50 (1989), pp. 468 - 482

CILIBERTI, ANNE C.; MARY F. CASSERLY; JUDITH L. HEGG; EUGENE S. MITCHELL: Material Availability: A Study of Academic Library Performance In: College and Research Libraries. - 48 (1987), pp. 513 - 527

CITRON, H. R.; J. B. DODD: Cost Allocation and Cost Recovery Considerations in a Special Academic Library: Georgia Institute of Technology In: Science and Technology Libraries. - 5 (1984), pp. 1 - 14

CLAPP, V. W.; R. T. JORDAN: Quantitative Criteria for Adequacy of Academic Library Collections
In: College and Research Libraries. - 26 (1965), pp. 371 - 380

CLARK, MAE M.: Evaluation of Searching
In: Acquisitions Librarian. - 6 (1991), pp. 131 - 147

CLARK, P. M.: A Study to Refine and Test New Measures for Library Service and Train Library Personnel in Their Use. - New Brunswick, N.J.: Rutgers, the State University, Bureau of Library and Information Science Research, 1976

CLEE, JAN; RUTH MAGUIRE: Library Environment and Library Usage
In: Library Management. - 14 (1993), pp. 6 - 8

CLOUSTAN, J.S.: How Much is Enough? Establishing a Corridor of Adequacy in Library Acquisitions
In: Collection Management. - 19 (1995), pp. 57 - 75

COALE, ROBERT P.: Evaluation of a Research Library Collection: Latin-American Colonial History at the Newberry
In: Library Quarterly. - 35 (1965), pp. 173 - 184

COHEN, LUCY R.: Conducting Performance Evaluations
In: Library Trends. - 38 (1989), pp. 40 - 52

COMER, C.: List-checking as a Method for Evaluating Library Collections
In: Collection Building. - 3 (1981), pp. 26 - 34

COOPER, W. S.: Expected Search Length: A Single Measure of Retrieval Effectiveness Based on the Weak Ordering Action of Retrieval Systems
In: American Documentation. - 19 (1968), pp. 30 - 41

COPE, CATHERINE: Performance Measurement in Libraries 1988-1990. - Loughborough: Loughborough University Library and Information Statistics Unit, 1990

CORVELLEC, HERVÉ: Évaluation des Performances des Bibliothèques: Tendances, Faiblesses et Perspectives
In: Bulletin des Bibliothèques de France. - 35 (1990), pp. 356 - 365

COSSETTE, ANDRÉ: Évaluation de l'Efficacité de la Bibliothèque: Analyse des Études Majeures
In: Documentation et Bibliothèques. - 24 (1978), pp. 115 - 128

COSTING AND THE ECONOMICS OF LIBRARY AND INFORMATION SERVICES / Ed. by S. A. Roberts. - London: ASLIB, 1984

COTTA-SCHØNBERG, MICHAEL; MAURICE B. LINE: Evaluation of Academic Libraries: With Special Reference to the Copenhagen Business School Library
In: Journal of Librarianship and Information Science. - 26 (1994), pp. 55 - 69

COUNCIL OF FEDERAL LIBRARIES: Performance Measurement in Federal Libraries: A Handbook. - Ottawa: National Library of Canada, 1979

CRAMER, S. A.: Management for Change in British University Libraries
In: Libri. - 27 (1977), pp. 68 - 83

CRAWFORD, GREGORY A.: A Conjoint Analysis of Reference Services in Academic Libraries
In: College and Research Libraries. - 55 (1994), pp. 257 - 267

CRAWFORD, JOHN C.: OPAC Satisfaction Survey, Glasgow Polytechnic, 10-14 February, 1992
In: COPOL Newsletter. - 61 (1993), pp. 49 - 56

CRAWFORD, JOHN C.; LINDA C. THOM ; JOHN A. POWLES: A Survey of Subject Access to Academic Library
Catalogues in Great Britain
In: Journal of Librarianship and Information Science. - 25 (1993), pp. 85 - 93

CRONIN, BLAISE: Performance Measurement and Information Management
In: ASLIB Proceedings. - 34 (1982), pp. 227 - 236

CRONIN, BLAISE: Taking the Measure of Service
In: ASLIB Proceedings. - 34 (1982), pp. 273 - 294

CRONIN, MARY J.: Performance Measurement for Public Services in Academic and Research Libraries. -
Washington, D.C.: Office of Managment Studies. Association of Research Libraries, 1985. - (Occasional Paper
; 9)

CROTTY, ANITA: Why Bother with Evaluation?
In: Library Acquisitions: Practice and Theory. - 18 (1994), pp. 51 - 56

CROWLEY, T.: Half-right Reference: Is it true?
In: RQ. - 25 (1985), pp. 59 - 68

CROWLEY, T.; THOMAS CHILDERS: Information Service in Public Libraries: Two Studies. - Metuchen, N.J.:
Scarecrow Press, 1971

CROWLEY, T.: Referred Reference Question: How Well Are They Answered
In: Evaluation of Reference Services / Ed. by W. Katz und R. A. Fraley. - New York, 1984, pp. 83 - 93

CUCHE, JEAN-LOUIS; DIACON LÖIC: Etudes d'usages et d'usagers: un example en Suisse Romande
In: ARBIDO-Revue. - 4 (1989), pp. 79 - 83

CULLEN, ROWENA J.; PHILIP J. CALVERT: Further Dimensions of Public Library Effectiveness: Report on a Parallel
New Zealand Study
In: Library and Information Science Research. - 15 (1993), pp. 143 - 164

DAIUTE, R. J.; K. A. GORMAN: Library Operations Research. - Dobbs Ferry, N.Y.: Oceana Publications, 1974

DALTON, GWENDA M.: Quantitative Approach to User Satisfaction in Reference Service Evaluation
In: Suid-Afrikaanse Tydskrif vir Biblioteek- en Inligtingkunde. - 60 (1992), pp. 89 - 103

DAVIES, ANNETTE; IAN KIRKPATRICK: To Measure Service
In: Library Association Record. - 96 (1994), pp. 88 - 89

DAVIS, MARY BYRD: Model for a Vendor Study in a Manual or Semi-automated Acquisitions System
In: Library Acquisitions: Practice and Theory. - 3 (1979), pp. 53 - 60

DAY, ABBY: Performance Indicators: The Librarian's Challenge
In: Library Management. - 11 (1990), pp. 24 - 28

DAY, MIKE; DON REVILL: Towards the Active Collection: The Use of Circulation Analyses in Collection Evaluation
In: Journal of Librarianship and Information Science. - 27 (1995), pp. 149 - 157

DE PROSPO, ERNEST R.: Performance Measures for Public Libraries. - Chicago: Public Library Association, 1973

D'ELIA, GEORGE; S. WALSH: Patrons' Uses and Evaluations of Library Services: A Comparison across Five Public Libraries
In: Library and Information Science Research. - 7 (1985), pp. 3 - 30

D'ELIA, GEORGE: Materials Availability Fill Rates - Useful Measures of Library Performance?
In: Public Libraries. - 24 (1985), pp. 106 - 110

DEPEW, JOHN N.: An Acquisitions Decision Model for Academic Libraries
In: Journal of the American Society for Information Science. - 26 (1975), pp. 237 - 246

DEPPING, RALF: Die availability study als Instrument bibliothekarischer Leistungsmessung
In: Bibliothek. Forschung und Praxis. - 18 (1994), pp. 20 - 40

DEPPING, RALF: Möglichkeiten und Grenzen des Leistungsvergleichs zwischen deutschen Universitätsbibliotheken
In: Bibliothek. Forschung und Praxis. - 18 (1994), pp. 312 - 322

DERIEZ, RENÉ; ELISABETH LE BARBANCHON: Le Circuit du Livre dans les Bibliothèques Universitaires: Évaluation des Tâches
In: Bulletin des Bibliothèques de France. - 38 (1993), pp. 50 - 54

DERIEZ, RENÉ; THIERRY GIAPPICONI: Analyser et Comparer les Coûts de Catalogage
In: Bulletin des Bibliothèques de France. - 39 (1994), pp. 28 - 33

DETWEILER, MARY JO: Availability of Materials in Public Libraries
In: Library Effectiveness: a State of the Art. - Chicago, 1980, pp. 75 - 83

DETWEILER, MARY JO: Planning - More than Progress
In: Library Journal. - 1 (1983), pp. 23 - 26

DICKSON, J.: An Analysis of User Errors in Searching an Online Catalog
In: Cataloging and Classification Quarterly. - 4 (1978), pp. 19 - 38

DIMATTIA, ERNEST A., JR: Total Quality Management and Servicing Users through Remote Access Technology
In: The Electronic Library. - 11 (1993), pp. 187 - 192

DIVILBISS, J. L.; P. C. SELF: Work Analysis by Simple Random Sampling
In: Bulletin of the Medical Library Association. - 66 (1978), pp. 19 - 23

DOELLING, DONNA L.: Blueprint for Performance Assessment
In: Medical Reference Services Quarterly. - 12 (1993), pp. 29 - 38

DOMAS, R. E.: Correlating the Classes of Books Taken Out Of and Books used Within an Open-Stack Library. - San Antonio: San Antonio College Library, 1978

DOUGHERTY, RICHARD M.: The Evaluation of Campus Library Document Delivery Service
In: College and Research Libraries. - 34 (1973), pp. 29 - 39

DOUGHERTY, RICHARD M.: Needed: User-responsive Research Libraries
In: Library Journal. - 1 (1991), pp. 59 - 62

DOWLIN, K.; L. MAGRATH: Beyond the Numbers: a Decision Support System
In: Library Automation as a Source of Management Information / Ed. by F. W. Lancaster. - Urbana, Ill., 1983, pp. 27 - 58

DuMont, Paul F.; Rosemary Ruhig-Dumont: Assessing the Effectiveness of Library Service. - Urbana, Ill.: Graduate School of Library and Information Science, 1981. - (University of Illinois, Graduate School of Library and Information Science, Occasional Papers ; 152)

DuMont, Paul F.; Rosemary Ruhig-Dumont: A Goal Typology and Systems Model of Library Effectiveness
In: Journal of Library Administration. - 2 (1981), pp. 13 - 23

Dyson, Rick; Kjestine Carey: User Preference for CD-ROMs: Implications for Library Planners
In: CD-ROM Professional. - 6 (1993), pp. 86 - 89

Easun, Sue: Beginner's Guide to Efficiency Measurement
In: School Library Media Quarterly. - 22 (1994), pp. 103 - 106

Eaton, Gale; Michael Vocino; Melanie Taylor: Evaluating Signs in a University Library
In: Collection Management. - 16 (1992), pp. 81-101

Eckwright, Gail Z.: Evaluating the Library BI Program
In: College and Research Libraries News. - 54 (1993), pp. 13 - 16

Edwards, E. Anne: Performance Evaluation of Collection Development and Acquisitions Librarians
In: Acquisitions Librarian. - 6 (1991), pp. 115 - 122

Die Effektive Bibliothek: Endbericht des Projekts "Anwendung und Erprobung einer Marketingkonzeption für öffentliche Bibliotheken" / Red. Peter Borchardt. - Berlin: Deutsches Bibliotheksinstitut (DBI-Materialien ; 119)

Elzy, Cheryl A.; F. W. Lancaster: Looking at a Collection in Different Ways: A Comparison of Methods of Bibliographic Checking
In: Collection Management. - 12 (1990), pp. 1 - 10

Elzy, Cheryl A.; Alan Nourie; F. W. Lancaster; Kurt M. Joseph: Evaluating Reference Service in a Large Academic Library
In: College and Research Libraries. - 52 (1991), pp. 454 - 465

Ephraim, P.E.: A Review of Qualitative and Quantitative Measures in Collection Analysis
In: The Electronic Library. - 12 (1994), pp. 237 - 241

Estabrook, L. S.: Valuing a Document Delivery System
In: RQ. - 26 (1986), pp. 58 - 62

Ettelt, Harold J.: Book Use at a Small (Very) Community College Library
In: Library Journal. - 103 (1978), pp. 2314 - 2315

Evans, Edward: Developing Library Collections. - Littleton, 1979

Evans, Edward; Harold Borko; Patricia Ferguson: Review of Criteria Used to Measure Library Effectiveness
In: Bulletin of the Medical Library Association. - 60 (1972), pp. 102 - 110

Evans, G. T.; A. Beilby: A Library Management Information System in a Multi-campus Environment
In: Library Automation as a Source of Management Information / Ed. by F. W. Lancaster. - Urbana, Ill., 1983, pp. 164 - 196

Farah, Barbara D.: Academic Reference Librarians: A Case for Self-evaluation
In: Reference Librarian. - 25/26 (1989), pp. 495 - 505

FERGUSON, ANTHONY W.: Collection Assessment and Acquisitions Budgets
In: Journal of Library Administration. - 17 (1992), pp. 59 - 70

FERL, TERRY ELLEN; LARRY MILLSAP: Remote Use of the University of California MELVYL Library System: An Online Survey
In: Information Technology and Libraries. - 11 (1992), pp. 285 - 303

FLEISHAUER, CAROL; MARILYN G. MCSWEENEY: Variations on a Theme: Evaluating the Acquisitions Department
In: Acquisitions Librarian. - 6 (1991), pp. 61 - 70

FLYNN, R.R.: The University of Pittsburgh Study of Journal Usage: A Summary Report
In: Serials Librarian. - 4 (1979), pp. 25 - 33

FORD, BARBARA J.; JOAN S. SEGAL: Measuring Academic Library Performance
In: International Federation of Library Associations and Institutions, 56th IFLA General Conference Stockholm, Sweden 18-24 August 1990, Booklet 1: Division of General Research Libraries. - Den Haag: IFLA, 1990, pp. 31 - 34

FORD, GEOFFREY: Approaches to Performance Measurement: Some Observations on Principles and Practice
In: British Journal of Academic Librarianship. - 4 (1989), pp. 74 - 87

FORD, GEOFFREY; ALAN MACDOUGALL: Performance Assessment in Academic Libraries: Final Report on a Feasibility Study. - London: British Library, 1992

FORD, GEOFFREY: Performance Measurements: Principles and Practice
In: IFLA Journal. - 15 (1989), pp. 13 - 17

FORD, GEOFFREY: Review of Methods Employed in Determining the Use of Library Stock. - London: British Library, 1990. - (British National Bibliography Research Fund Report ; 43)

FRALEY, RUTH: Publishers vs. Wholesalers: The Ordering Dilemma
In: Library Acquisitions: Practice and Theory. - 3 (1979), pp. 9 - 13

FRENCH, BEVERLEE: Library Performance Measures
In: College and Research Libraries News. - 48 (1987), pp. 72 - 74

FROHMBERG, K. A.: Increases in Book Availability in a Large College Library
In: Proceedings of the American Society for Information Science. - 17 (1980), pp. 292 - 294

FUSSLER, H. H.; J. L. SIMON: Patterns in the Use of Books in Large Research Libraries. - Chicago: University of Chicago Press, 1969

FUTAS, ELIZABETH: The Role of Public Services in Collection Evaluation
In: Library Trends. - 33 (1985), pp. 397 - 399

GABRIEL, M. R.: Online Collection Evaluation: Course by Course
In: Collection Building. - 8 (1987), pp. 20 - 24

GAILLARD, CATHERINE: Tableau de Bord à la Bibliothèque de l'Université de Paris 6
In: Bulletin des Bibliothèques de France. - 35 (1990), pp. 302 - 304

GALVIN, THOMAS J.; ALLEN KENT: Use of a University Library Collection: A Progress Report on a Pittsburgh study
In: Library Journal. - 102 (1977), pp. 2317 - 2320

GASKILL, H. V.; R. M. DUNBAR; C.H. BROWN: An Analytical Study of the Use of a College Library
In: Library Quarterly. - 4 (1934), pp. 564 - 586

GAYLOR, R.H.: Collection Analysis at a Junior College Library: The OCLC/Amigos CACD
In: OCLC Systems and Services. - 10 (1994), pp. 9 - 12

GERS, R.; L. J. SEWARD: Improving Reference Performance: Results of a Statewide Study
In: Library Journal. - 110 (1985), pp. 32 - 35

GETZ, MALCOLM: Analysis and Library Management
In: Academic libraries: Research Perspectives / Ed. by Mary Jo Lynch. - Chicago, 1990. - (ACRL Publications in Librarianship; 47), pp. 192 - 214

GIAPPICONI, THIERRY: Library Evaluation and Public Policy: A French View
In: Journal of Librarianship and Information Science. - 27 (1995), pp. 99 - 108

GILBERT, J. D.: Het project kwaliteitsverbetering: keerpunt in de ontwikkeling van de Universiteitsbibliotheek van de Rijksuniversiteit Limburg
In: Bibliotheken: tot uw dienst / Red.: Henk van de Hoogen, Marianne de Ruwe. - Assen: Van Gorcum, 1992, pp. 7 - 24

GILLENTINE, J.: Evaluating Library Services. - Santa Fe: New Mexico State Library, 1981

GOEHLERT, R.: Book Availability and Delivery Service
In: Journal of Academic Librarianship. - 4 (1978), pp. 368 - 371

GOLDEN, B.: A Method for Quantitatively Evaluating a University Library Collection
In: Library Resources and Technical Services. - 18 (1974), pp. 268 - 274

GOLDHOR, HERBERT: Analysis of an Inductive Method of Evaluating the Book Collection of a Public Library
In: Libri. - 23 (1973), pp. 6 - 17

GOODALL, DEBORAH L.: Performance Measurement: A Historical Perspective
In: Journal of Librarianship. - 20 (1988), pp. 128 - 144

GORDON, JANET L: Measuring Supplier Performance
In: Library Acquisitions: Theory and Practice, 18 (1994), pp. 67-70

GORE, D.: Let Them Eat Cake while Reading Catalog Cards: An Essay on the Availability Problem
In: Library Journal. - 100 (1975), pp. 93 - 98

GORMAN, G. E.; B. R. HOWES: Collection Development for Libraries. - London: Bowker - Saur, 1989 (Topics in Library and Information Studies)

GOTHBERG, HELEN M.: The Library Survey: A Research Methodology Rediscovered
In: College and Research Libraries. - 51 (1990), pp. 555 - 559

GOUKE, M. N.; PEASE S.: Title Searches in an Online Catalog and a Card Catalog
In: Journal of Academic Librarianship. - 8 (1982), pp. 137 - 143

GRANT, JOAN; SUSAN PERELMUTER: Vendor Performance Evaluation
In: Journal of Academic Librarianship. - 4 (1978), pp. 366 - 367

GUDAUSKAS, RENALDAS; RUDZIONIENE, JURGITA: Library Performance Measurement at the Vilnius University Library
In: Library Management Development Projekt. 3rd Report - Preliminary. - Stockholm: Universitetsbibliotek, 1995, pp. 19 - 29

GUIDE TO PERFORMANCE EVALUATION OF LIBRARY MATERIALS VENDORS / Ed. by the Management and Development Committee and the Acquisitions Committee, Resources Section, Resources and Technical Services Division, American Library Association. - Chicago: American Library Association, 1988

GUIDELINES FOR COLLEGE LIBRARIES: RECOMMENDATIONS FOR PERFORMANCE AND RESOURCING / ed. by Kathy Ennis. - 5th ed. . - London: Library Association Publishing, 1995

HALL, BLAINE H.: Collection Assessment Manual for College and University Libraries. - Phoenix: Oryx Press, 1985

HALL, BLAINE H.: Writing the Collection Assessment Manual
In: Collection Management. - 6 (1984), pp. 49 - 61

HAMAKER, CHARLES A.: Some Measures of Cost Effectiveness in Library Collections
In: Journal of Library Administration. - 16 (1992), pp. 57-69

HAMBURG, M.: Library Planning and Decision-Making Systems. - Cambridge, Mass.: MIT Press, 1974

HANCOCK-BEAULIEU, MICHELINE STEPHEN ROBERTSON, COLIN NEILSON: Evaluation of Online Catalogues: An Assessment of Methods. - London: British Library. Research and Develoment Department, 1990. - (Research Paper ; 78)

HANNABUS, STUART: The Importance of Performance Measures
In: Library Review. - 36 (1987), pp. 248 - 253

HANNABUS, STUART: Introduction to Performance Measures: Selected Teaching Examples
In: Information and Library Manager. - 7 (1987), pp. 31 - 37

HANNABUS, STUART: Probability and Expectation
In: Information and Library Manager. - 9 (1990), pp. 10 - 12

HARMAN, DONNA: Evaluation Issues in Information Retrieval
In: Information Processing and Management. - 28 (1992), pp. 439 - 528

HARRIS, C.: A Comparison of Issues and In-library Use of Books
In: ASLIB Proceedings. - 29 (1977), pp. 118 - 126

HARRIS, I. W.: The Influence of Accessibility on Academic Library Use. - New Brunswick, Rutgers, The State University, Diss., 1966

HARRIS, MELANIE: The User Survey in Performance Measurement
In: British Journal of Academic Librarianship. - 6 (1991), pp. 1 - 12

HARRIS, PATRICIA R.: The Development of International Standards: Exploring the ISO/IFLA Relationship
In: IFLA Journal. - 17 (1991), pp. 358 - 365

HAWTHORN, MARGARET; ELAINE GOETTLER: Proportionate Probability Sampling: A Technique to Find Out the Needs of Library Users and Nonusers
In: College and Research Libraries. - 54 (1993), pp. 322 - 324

HAYES, R. M.: The Distribution of Use of Library Materials: Analysis of Data from the University of Pittsburgh
In: Library Research. - 3 (1981), pp. 215 - 260

HENDERSON, WILLIAM ABBOT; WILLIAM J. HUBBARD; SONJA L. MCABEE: Collection Assessment in Academic
Libraries: Institutional Effectiveness in Microcosm
In: Library Acquisitions: Practice and Theory. - 17 (1993), pp. 197 - 201

HENDRICKSON, KENT: Standards for University Libraries: Evaluation of Performance
In: College and Research Libraries News. - 50 (1989), pp. 679 - 691

HENTY, MARGARET: Performance Indicators in Higher Education Libraries
In: British Journal of Academic Librarianship. - 4 (1989), pp. 177 - 191

HERNON, PETER; ELLEN ALTMAN: Service Quality in Academic Libraries. - Norwood, N.J.: Ablex, 1995

HERNON, PETER; CHARLES R. MCCLURE: Evaluation and Library Decision Making. - Norwood, N.J.: Ablex, 1990. -
(Information Management, Policy, and Services Series)

HERNON, PETER; CHARLES R. MCCLURE: Library Reference Service: An Unrecognized Crisis - A Symposium
In: Journal of Academic Librarianship. - 13 (1987), pp. 69 - 71

HERNON, PETER; CHARLES R. MCCLURE: Quality of Data Issues in Unobtrusive Testing of Library Reference
Service: Recommendations and Strategies
In: Library and Information Science Research. - 9 (1987), pp. 77 - 93

HERNON, PETER; CHARLES R. MCCLURE: Unobtrusive Testing and Library Reference Services. - Norwood, N.J.:
Ablex, 1987

HINDLE, ANTHONY; MICHAEL K. BUCKLAND: In-library Book Usage in Relation to Circulation
In: Collection Management. - 2 (1978), pp. 265 - 277

HISCOCK, JANE E.: Does Library Usage affect Academic Performance?
In: Australian Academic and Research Libraries. - 17 (1986), pp. 207-213

HOED, WILLEM DEN: Kwantitatieve evaluatiemethode legt onevenwichtigheden in de collectie bloot: populariteit
van genres en rubrieken statistisch onderbouwd
In: Bibliotheek en Samenleving. - 19 (1991), pp. 189 - 192

HÖGLUND, ANNA-LENA: Measure the Performance of Public Libraries and Your Planning Will Be Easier, More
Rewarding - and More Successful
In: International Library Review. - 23 (1991), pp. 31 - 47

HOFMANN, ULRICH: Wirtschaftlichkeit in Bibliotheken: neue Konzepte notwendig
In: Bibliotheksdienst. - 26 (1992), pp. 1178 - 1184

HUMPHREYS, K.W.: Standards in University Libraries
In: Libri. - 20 (1970), pp. 144 - 155

HUNT, C. J.: Library Reviews
In: British Journal of Academic Librarianship. - 5 (1990), pp. 135 - 140

HYMAN, FERNE B.: Collection Evaluation in the Research Library
In: Collection Building. - 9 (1989), pp. 33 - 37

IFIDON, SAM E.: The Evaluation of Performance
In: Libri. - 36 (1986), pp. 224 - 239

IFLA INTERNATIONAL OFFICE FOR UAP: Measuring the Performance of Document Supply Systems. - Paris: UNESCO, 1987

INTNER, SHEILA S.: Responsibilities of Technical Service Librarians to the Process of Collection Evaluation
In: Library Trends. - 33 (1985), pp. 417 - 436

ISO 9004-2 : 1991. Quality Management and Quality System Elements - Part 2: Guidelines for Services

JACOBS, N.A.; R.C. YOUNG: Measuring Book Availability in an Academic Library: A Methodological Comparison
In: Journal of Documentation, 51 (1995), pp. 281 - 290

JAGER, KARIN DE: Library Use and Academic Achievement
In: Proceedings of the 1st Northumbria International Conference on Performance Measurement in Libraries and Information Services / Edited Pat Wressell. - Newcastle upon Tyne: Information North, 1995, p. 287

JAGER, KARIN DE: Obsolescence and Stress: A Study of the Use of Books on Open Shelves at a University Library
In: Journal of Librarianship and Information Science. - 26 (1994), pp. 71 - 81.

JAIN, A. K.: Report on a Statistical Study of Book Use. - Lafayette, Ind.: Purdue University, School of Industrial Engineering, 1967

JAIN, A. K.: A Sampled Data Study of Book Usage in the Purdue University Libraries. - Lafayette, Ind.: Purdue University, 1965

JAIN, A. K.: Sampling and Data Collection Methods for a Book-use Study
In: Library Quarterly. - 39 (1969), pp. 245 - 252

JAIN, A. K.: Sampling and Short-period Usage in the Purdue Library
In: College and Research Libraries. - 27 (1966), pp. 211 - 218

JARDINE, CAROLYN W.: Maybe the 55 Percent Rule Doesn't Tell the Whole Story: A User-Satisfaction Survey
In: College and Research Libraries. - 56 (1995), pp. 477 - 485

JARVIS, KEN: Not Just Books - A Survey of Whole Library Use
In: Library and Information Research News. - 13 (1990), pp. 9 - 12

JENKS, G. M.: Circulation and Its Relationship to the Book Collection and Academic Departments
In: College and Research Libraries. - 37 (1976), pp. 145 - 152

JOHNSON, C. A.; R. W. TRUESWELL: The Weighted Criteria Statistic Score: An Approach to Journal Selection
In: College and Research Libraries. - 39 (1978), pp. 287 - 292

JOHNSON, HEATHER: Strategic Planning for Modern Libraries
In: Library Management. - 15 (1994), pp. 7 - 18

JOHNSON, STEVEN D.: Rush Processing
In: Journal of Academic Librarianship, 11 (1985), pp. 345-348

KANIA, ANTOINETTE M.: Academic Library Standards and Performance Measures
In: College and Research Libraries. - 49 (1988), pp. 16 - 23

KANTOR, PAUL B.: Availability Analysis
In: Journal of the American Society for Information Science. - 27 (1976), pp. 311 - 319

KANTOR, PAUL B.: Demand-adjusted Shelf Availability Parameters
In: Journal of Academic Librarianship. - 7 (1981), pp. 78 - 82

KANTOR, PAUL B.: The Library as an Information Utility in the University Context: Evolution and Measurement of Service
In: Journal of the American Society for Information Science. - 27 (1976), pp. 100 - 112

KANTOR, PAUL B.: Library Cost Analysis
In: Library Trends. - 38 (1989), pp. 171 - 188

KANTOR, PAUL B.: Objective Performance Measures for Academic and Research Libraries. - Washington, D.C.: Association of Research Libraries, 1984

KANTOR, PAUL B.: Vitality: An Indirect Measure of Relevance
In: Collection Management. - 2 (1978), pp. 83 - 95

KASKE, N. K.; N. P. SANDERS: Study of Online Public Access Catalogs: an Overview and Application of Findings. - Dublin, Ohio: Online Computer Library Center, 1983

KELLEY, PATRICIA M.: Performance Measures: A Tool for Planning Resource Allocations
In: Journal of Library Administration. - 14 (1991), pp. 21 - 36

KENDRICK, CURTIS L.: Performance Measures of Shelving Accuracy
In: Journal of Academic Librarianship. - 17 (1991), pp. 16 - 18

KENT, ALLEN: Use of Library Materials: The University of Pittsburgh Study. - New York: Dekker, 1979

KFLU, TESFAI: Vendor Performance Evaluation: Numeric Formula
In: Library Acquisitions: Practice and Theory. - 14 (1990), pp. 307 - 312

KIDSTON, JAMES S.: The Validity of Questionnaire Responses
In: Library Quarterly. - 55 (1985), pp. 133 - 150

KILGOUR, FREDERICK G.: Recorded Use of Books in the Yale Medical Library
In: American Documentation. - 12 (1961), pp. 266 - 269

KILGOUR, FREDERICK G.: Toward 100 Percent Availability
In: Library Journal. - 15 (1989), pp. 50 - 53

KING EVANS, JOSEPHINE: Tracking Perodical Usage in a Research Library
In: College and Research Libraries News. - 51 (1990), pp. 958 - 959

KING, G. B.; R. BERRY: Evaluation of the University of Minnesota Libraries Reference Department Telephone Information Service: Pilot Study. - Minneapolis: University of Minnesota, Library School, 1973

KING, GERALDINE B.: Performance Appraisal in the Automated Environment
In: Journal of Library Administration. - 13 (1991), pp. 195 - 204

KING, NATALIE SCHOCH: Search Characteristics and the Effects of Experience on End Users of PaperChase
In: College and Research Libraries. - 52 (1991), pp. 360 - 374

KINGMA, J.; L. A. F. M. KERKLAAN: Kwaliteit in de zakelijke dienstverlening: de kwaliteitsbalans als een instrument voor zelfdiagnose
In: Bibliotheek en Samenleving. - 19 (1991), pp. 232 - 234

KINNELL, MARGARET: Quality Mangement and Library and Information Services: Competetive Advantage for the Information Revolution
In: IFLA Journal. - 21 (1995), pp. 265 - 273

KIRK, ROY: What Do Our Readers Want? Some Conclusions from a Survey made at Leicester University Library: An Education Library Slant
In: Education Libraries Journal. - 38 (1995), pp. 5 - 16

KNUTSON, GUNNAR: A Comparison of Online and Card Catalog Accuracy
In: Library Resources and Technical Services. - 34 (1990), pp. 24 - 35

KOCK, MARTHIE DE: Remote Users of an Online Public Access Catalogue (OPAC): Problems and Support
In: The Electronic Library. - 11 (1993), pp. 241 - 243

KOKKONEN, OILI: Toiminnan arviointi käynnistetään Ruotsin korkeakoulukirjastoissa [Measur-ing university library performance has started in Sweden]
In: Signum. - 24 (1991), pp. 179 - 182

KOLNER, STUART J.; ERIC C. WELCH: The Book Availability Study as an Objective Measure of Performance in a Health Science Library
In: Bulletin of the Medical Library Association. - 73 (1985), pp. 121 - 131

KOSKIALA, SINIKKA: Measuring the Performance of Academic Libraries in Finland.
In: IATUL Proceedings (New Series). - 3 (1994), pp. 62 - 74

KOSKIALA, SINIKKA: Performance Measures for Finnish University Libraries
In: Quality Issues in the Library and Information Services: Proceedings of a Conference Organised by NORD-INFO and the British Library (Research and Development Department). Held at Hässelby Slott, Stockholm, Sweden, 8-10 October 1993. - Esbo: NORDINFO, 1994, pp. 95 - 106

KROLL, H. REBECCA: Beyond Evaluation: Performance Appraisal as a Planning and Motivational Tool in Libraries
In: Journal of Academic Librarianship. - 9 (1983), pp. 27 - 32

KRUEGER, K.: Coordinated Cooperative Collection Development for Illinois Libraries. - Vols. 1- 3. - Springfield: Illinois State Library, 1983

KUPIEC, A.W. ET AL.: Bibliothèques et Evaluation. - Paris: Editions du Cercle de la Librairie, 1994

LANCASTER, F. W.: Evaluating Collections by Their Use
In: Collection Management. - 4 (1982), pp. 15 - 43

LANCASTER, F. WILFRID: If You Want to Evaluate Your Library ... - 2nd. ed. - Champaign, Ill.: University of Illinois, Graduate School of Library and Information Science, 1993

LANCASTER, F. W.: Information Retrieval Systems: Characteristics, Testing and Evaluation / F. Wilfrid Lancaster. - 2nd ed. - New York: Wiley, 1979

LANCASTER, F. W., SHARON L. BAKER: The Measurement and Evaluation of Library Services. - 2nd ed. - Arlington, Vir.: Information Resources Press, 1991

LANCASTER, F. W.; R. MEHROTRA: The Five Laws of Library Science as a Guide to the Evaluation of Library Services
In: Perspectives in Library and Information Science. - Vol. 1. - Lucknow, 1982, pp. 26 - 39

LANDESMAN, MARGARET; CHRISTOPHER GATES: Performance of American In-print Vendors: A Comparison at the University of Utah
In: Library Acquisitions: Practice and Theory. - 4 (1980), pp.187 - 192

LANE, DAVID O.: The Selection of Academic Library Materials: A Literature Survey
In: College and Research Libraries. - 29 (1968), pp. 364 - 372

LANE, LORRAINE M.: The Relationship between Loans and In-house Use of Books in Determining a Use-factor for Budget Allocation
In: Library Acquisitions: Practice and Theory. - 11 (1987), pp. 95 - 102

LAPÈLERIE, FRANCOIS: L'Évaluation d'une Bibliothèque par la Méthode de Kantor
In: Bulletin des Bibliothèques de France. - 39 (1994), pp. 55 - 66

LAWSON, CLINTON D.: Where in Hell Are the Books We Ordered?: A Study of Speed of Service from Canadian Publishers
In: Ontario Library Review. - 55 (1971), pp. 237 - 241

LEMMINK, J. G. A. M.: Kwaliteitsmetingen in een universiteitsbibliotheek: een noodzakelijke focus op klant en medewerker
In: Bibliotheken: tot uw dienst / Red.: Henk van den Hoogen, Marianne de Ruwe. - Assen: Van Gorcum, 1992.

LEONARD, LAWRENCE E.; JOAN M. MAIER; RICHARD M. DOUGHERTY: Centralized Book Processing: A Feasibility Study Based on Colorado Academic Libraries. - Metuchen, N.J.: The Scarecrow Press, 1969

LEVINE, MARILYN M.: The Circulation/Acquisition Ratio: An Input-Output Measure for Libraries
In: Information Processing and Management. - 16 (1980), pp. 313 - 315

LEWIS, DAVID W.: Research on the Use of Online Catalogs and Its Implications for Library Practice
In: Journal of Academic Librarianship. - 13 (1987), pp. 152 - 157

LEWIS, DAVID W.: An Organizational Paradigm for Effective Academic libraries
In: College and Research Libraries. - 47 (1986), pp. 337 - 353

LIBOIRON, PIERRE R.: L'Évaluation des Collections: Les Fondements
In: Argus. - 19 (1990), pp. 3 - 10

LIBRARY PERFORMANCE MEASUREMENT: ANSVARSBIBLIOTEKENES UNDERSØKELSE AV FJERNKOPITJENESTEN / Styringsgruppen for Ansvarsbibliotek i Norge. - Oslo. Universitetsbibliotekets trykkeri, 1993. - (Skrifter fra Riksbiblioteksjenesten ; 63)

LIBRARY PROVISION IN HIGHER EDUCATION INSTITUTION / Ed. by Higher Education Council. - National Board of Employment, Education and Training, 1990. - (Commissioned Report ; 7)

LIDMAN, TOMAS; TÖRNGREN, MARGARETA: Case study at the Stockholm University Library (RUT)
In: INSPEL. - 28 (1994), pp. 55 - 66

LINE, MAURICE B.: The Ability of a University Library to Provide Books Wanted by Researchers
In: Journal of Librarianship. - 5 (1973), pp. 37 - 51

LINE, MAURICE B.: The Concept of "Library Goodness": User and Library Perception of Quality and Value
In: Academic Library Management: Edited Papers of a British Council Sponsored Course, 15 - 27 January 1989, Birmingham / Ed. by Maurice B. Line. - London: Library Association, 1990, pp. 185 - 195

LINE, MAURICE B.: Current Issues in Academic Libraries
In: Academic Library Management: Edited Papers of a British Council Sponsored Course, 15 - 27 January 1989, Birmingham / Ed. by Maurice B. Line. - London: Library Association, 1990, pp. 1 - 6

LINE, MAURICE B.: Performance Measurement within Interlending and Document Supply Systems
In: Interlending and Document Supply: Proceedings of the Second International Conference, London Nov. 1990 / International Conference on Interlending and Document Supply. - Southampton, 1991, pp. 5 - 13

LINE, MAURICE B.: Rank Lists based on Citations and Library Uses as Indicators of Journal Usage in Individual Libraries
In: Collection Management. - 2 (1978), pp. 313 - 316

LINE, MAURICE B.; A. SANDISON: "Obsolescence" and Changes in the Use of Literature with Time
In: Journal of Documentation. - 30 (1974), pp. 283 - 350

LINES, LIZ: Performance Measurement in Academic Libraries: A University Perspective
In: British Journal of Academic Librarianship. - 4 (1989), pp. 111 - 120

LIPETZ, BEN-AMI: Catalog Use in a Large Research Library
In: Library Quarterly. - 42 (1972), pp. 129 - 139

LIPETZ, BEN-AMI; P. J. PAULSON: A Study of the Impact of Introducing an Online Subject Catalog at the New York State Library
In: Library Trends. - 35 (1987), pp. 597 - 617

LIPETZ, BEN-AMI: User Requirements in Identifying Desired Works in a Large Library. - New Haven: Yale University Library, 1970

LOFGREN, HANS: Priority and Performance Evaluation: A Tool for Libraries
In: The Australian Library Journal. - 41 (1992), pp. 14 - 30

LOPEZ, M. D.: The Lopez or Citation Technique of In-depth Collection Evaluation Explicated
In: College and Research Libraries. - 44 (1983), pp. 251 - 255

LOR, PETER J.: Measuring the Outcomes of Southern African Interlending Requests: A Comparison of Measurement Approaches
In: Suid-Afrikaanse Tydskrif vir Biblioteek- en Inligtingkunde. - 57 (1989), pp. 362 - 371

LOSEE, ROBERT M.: Information in Data Collection: Models of Database and Library Quality
In: Journal of the American Society for Information Science. - 41 (1990). p. 359 - 367

LUND, PATRICIA A.: Measuring Turnaround Time in a Public Library System
In: Journal of Interlibrary Loan & Information Supply. - 1 (1991), pp. 31- 52

LYNCH, BEVERLY P.: University Library Standardq
In: Library Trends. - 31 (1982), pp. 33 - 47

LYNCH, MARY JO: Measurement of Library Output: How Is It Related to Research?
In: Library Performance, Accountability and Responsiveness: Essays in Honor of Ernest R. DeProspo / Ed. by Charles C. Curran and F. William Summers. - Norwood, 1990, pp. 1 - 8

MACDOUGALL, ALAN: Performance Assessment: Today's Confusion, Tomorrows Solution?
In: IFLA Journal. - 17 (1991), pp. 371 - 378

MACKENZIE, A. GRAHAM: Performance Measurement
In: Academic Library Management: Edited Papers of a British Council Sponsored Course, 15-27 January 1989, Birmingham / Ed. by Maurice Line. - London: Library Association, 1990, pp. 196 - 205

MAGRILL, ROSE MARY; JOHN CORBIN: Acquisitions Management and Collection Development in Libraries. - 2nd ed. - Chicago: American Library Association, 1989

MAGSON, M. S.: Techniques for the Measurement of Cost-benefit in Information Centres
In: ASLIB Proceedings. - 25 (1973), pp. 164 - 185

MAGUIRE, CARMEL; PATRICIA WILLARD: Performance Measures for Libraries: Statistical, Organisational and Cosmetic
In: Australian Academic and Research Libraries. - 21 (1990), pp. 262 - 273

MALTBY, A.: Measuring Catalogue Utility
In: Journal of Librarianship. - 3 (1971), pp. 180 - 189

MALTBY, A.: U.K. Catalogue Use Survey. - London: The Library Association, 1973. - (Library Association Research Publication ; 12)

MANKIN, C. J.; J. D. BASTILLE: An Analysis of the Differences Between Density-of-use Ranking and Raw-use Ranking of Library Journal Use
In: Journal of the American Society for Information Science. - 32 (1981), pp. 224 - 228

MANSBRIDGE, JOHN: Availability Studies in Libraries
In: Library and Information Science Research. - 8 (1986), pp. 299 - 314

MANSBRIDGE, JOHN: Evaluating Resource Sharing Library Networks. - Cleveland: Case Western Reserve University, Diss., 1984

MANSFIELD, JERRY W.: Human Factors of Queuing: A Library Circulation Model
In: Journal of Academic Librarianship. - 6 (1981), pp. 342 - 344

MARKEY, KAREN: The Process of Subject Searching in the Library Catalog: Final Report of the Subject Access Research Project. - Dublin, Ohio: Online Computer Library Center, 1983

MARKEY, KAREN: Subject Searching in Library Catalogs. - Dublin, Ohio: Online Computer Library Center, 1984

MARTYN, JOHN; F. W. LANCASTER: Investigative Methods in Library and Information Science: An Introduction. - Arlington, Vir.: Information Resources Press, 1981

MATHIESON, KIERAN: Measuring User's Beliefs About Information Systems: Techniques for Improving Accuracy
In: Encyclopedia of Library and Information Science / Ed. Allen Kent. - Vol. 56, Suppl. 19. - New York: Dekker, 1995, pp. 249 - 260

MCCARTHY, CHERYL ANN: Students' Perceived Effectiveness Using the University Library
In: College and Research Libraries. - 56 (1995), pp. 221 - 234

MCCLURE, CHARLES R.: Integrating Performance Measures into the Planning Process: Moving toward Decision Support Systems
In: Library Performance, Accountability and Responsiveness: Essays in Honor of Ernest R. DeProspo / Ed. by Charles C. Curran and F. Williams Summers. - Norwood, N.J.: Ablex, 1990, pp. 17 - 32

MCCLURE, CHARLES R.: A View from the Trenches: Costing and Performance Measures for Academic Library Public Services
In: College and Research Libraries. - 47 (1986), pp. 323 - 336

MCCLURE, CHARLES R.; ALAN R. SAMUELS: Factors Affecting the Use of Information for Academic Library Decision Making
In: College and Research Libraries. - 46 (1985), pp. 483 - 498

MCCLURE, CHARLES R.; CYNTHIA LOPATO: Performance Measures for the Academic Networked Environment
In: Proceedings of the 1st Northumbria International Conference on Performance Measurement in Libraries and Information Services / Edited Pat Wressell. - Newcastle upon Tyne: Information North, 1995, pp. 63 - 73.

MCCLURE, CHARLES R.; PETER HERNON: Improving the Quality of Reference Service for Government Publications. - Chicago: American Library Association, 1983

MCCLURE, CHARLES R.; PETER HERNON: Unobtrusive Testing and the Role of Library Management
In: Reference Librarian. - 18 (1987), pp. 71 - 85

MCCLURE, CHARLES R.; DOUGLAS L. ZWEIZIG; NANCY A. VANHOUSE; MARY JO LYNCH: Output Measures: Myths, Realities, and Prospects
In: Public Libraries. - 25 (1986), pp. 49 - 52

MCCREIGHT, JO ANN O.: Is the Sky Falling? or Using the Policies and Procedures Manual as an Evaluation Tool
In: Reference Librarian. - 38 (1992), pp. 251 - 255

MCDONALD, DAVID R.; MARGARET W. MAXFIELD; VIRGINIA G. F. FRIESNER: Sequential Analysis: A Methodology for Monitoring Approval Plans
In: College and Research Libraries. - 40 (1979) - p. 329 - 334

MCDONALD, JOSEPH A.; LYNDA BASNEY MICIKAS: Academic Libraries: The Dimensions of Their Effectiveness. - Westport, Conn.: Greenwood, 1994

MCELROY, A. R.: Standards and Guidelines in Performance Measurement
In: British Journal of Academic Librarianship. - 4 (1989), pp. 88 - 98

MCGRATH, WILLIAM E.: Collection Evaluation: Theory and the Search for Structure
In: Library Trends. - 33 (1985), pp. 241 - 266

MCGRATH, WILLIAM E.: Correlating the Subjects of Books Taken Out of and Books Used Within an Open-Stack Library
In: College and Research Libraries. - 32 (1971), pp. 280 - 285

MCGRATH, WILLIAM E.: Measuring Classified Circulation according to Curriculum
In: College and Research Libraries. - 29 (1968), pp. 347 - 350

MCGRATH, WILLIAM E.: Relationships between Hard/Soft, Pure/Applied, and Life/Nonlife Disciplines and Subject Book Use in a University Library
In: Information Processing and Management. - 14 (1978), pp. 17 - 28

MCGRATH, WILLIAM E.: The Significance of Books Used according to a Classified Profile of Academic Departments
In: College and Research Libraries. - 23 (1972), pp. 212 - 219

MCLEAN, NEIL; CLARE WILDE: Evaluating Library Performance: The Search for Relevance
In: Australian Academic and Research Libraries. - 22 (1991), pp. 198 - 217

MCMURDO, GEORGE: User Satisfaction
In: New Library World. - 81 (1980), pp. 83 - 85

MCNALLY, PETER F.: Teaching Performance Measurement for Reference Service
In: The Reference Librarian. - 25/26 (1989), pp. 591 - 600

METZ, P.: Duplication in Library Collections: What We Know and What We Need to Know
In: Collection Building. - 2 (1980), pp. 27 - 33

METZ, PAUL: The Landscape of Literatures: Use of Subject Collections in a Library. - Chicago: American Library Association, 1983. - (ACRL Publications in Librarianship ; 43)

MIDWINTER, ARTHUR; MURRAY MCVICAR: Public Libraries and Performance Indicators: Origins, Developments and Issues
In: Library Review. - 39 (1990), pp. 10 - 22

MIIL, KÄRT; TOONEV, URVE; IIUS, MARE ET AL.: Library Performance Measurement at Tartu University Library
In: Library Management Development Projekt. 3rd Report - Preliminary. - Stockholm: Universitetsbibliotek, 1995, pp. 30 - 67

MILLER, ARTHUR H.: Do the Books We Buy Get Used?
In: Collection Management. - 12 (1990), pp. 15 - 20

MILLER, RUTH H.; MARTHA W. NIEMEIER: Vendor Performance: A Study of Two Libraries
In: Library Resources and Technical Services. - 31 (1987), pp. 60 - 68

MILNE, DOROTHY; BILL TIFFANY: A Cost-per-use Method for Evaluating the Cost-effectiveness of Serials: A Detailed Discussion of Methodology
In: Serials Review. - 17 (1991), pp. 7 - 19

MILLSAP, LARRY; TERRY ELLEN FERL: Search Patters of Remote Users: An Analysis of OPAC Transaction Logs
In: Information Technology and Libraries. - 12 (1993), pp. 321 - 343

MILLSON-MARTULA, CHRISTOPHER; VANAJA MENON: Customer Expectations: Concepts and Reality for Academic Library Services
In: College and Research Libraries. - 56 (1995), pp. 33 - 47

MITCHELL, EUGENE S.; MARIE L. RADFORD; JUDITH L. HEGG: Book Availability: Academic Library Assessment
In: College and Research Libraries. - 55 (1994), pp. 47 - 55

MOORE, CAROLE WEISS: User Reactions to Online Catalogs: An Exploratory Study
In: College and Research Libraries. - 42 (1981), pp. 295 - 302

MOORE, MATTHEWS S.: Measuring and Managing Circulation Activity Using Circulation Rates
In: Collection Management. - 17 (1992), pp. 193 - 216

MORGAN, STEVE: Performance Assessment in Academic Libraries. - London: Mansell Pub, 1995

MORGAN, STEVE: Performance Assessment in Higher Education Libraries
In: Library Management. - 14 (1993), pp. 35 - 42

MORRIS, DILYS E.: Staff Time and Costs for Cataloguing
In: Library Resources and Technical Services. - 36 (1992), pp. 79 - 95

MORSE, PHILIP M.: Demand for Library Materials: An Exercise in Probability Analysis
In: Collection Management. - 1 (1976), pp. 47 - 78

MORSE, PHILIP M.: Library Effectiveness: A Systems Approach. - Cambridge (Mass.): Massachusetts Institute of Technology Press, 1968

MORSE, PHILIP M.: Measures of Library Effectiveness
In: Library Quarterly. - 42 (1972), pp. 15 - 30

MORSE, PHILIP M.; CHINGH-CHIH CHEN: Using Circulation Desk Data to Obtain Unbiased Estimates of Book Use
In: In: Library Quarterly. - 45 (1975), pp. 179 - 194

MOSHER, PAUL H.: Collection Evaluation in Research Libraries: The Search for Quality, Consistency, and System in Collection Development
In: Library Resources and Technical Services. - 23 (1979), pp. 16 - 32

MOSHER, PAUL H.: Quality and Library Collections: New Directions in Research and Practice in Collection Evaluation
In: Advances in Librarianship. - 13 (1984), pp. 211 - 238

MOSTYN, GREGORY R.: The Use of Supply-demand Equality in Evaluating Collection Adequacy
In: Californian Librarian. - 35 (1974), pp. 16 - 23

MUELLER, ELIZABETH; RALPH SCHMIDT; WERNER SCHWUCHOW: Are New Books Read More than Old Ones?
In: Library Quarterly. - 35 (1965), pp. 166 - 172

MÜLLER, RAYMUND: Qualitative und quantitative Aspekte der Wirtschaftlichkeit von Informationsdienstleistungen
In: Nachrichten für Dokumentation. - 41 (1990), pp. 175 - 183

MURFIN, M. E.: Evaluation of Reference Service by User Report of Success
In: Reference Librarian. - 49/50 (1995), pp. 229 - 241

MURFIN, M. E.: The Myth of Accessibility: Frustration and Failure in Retrieving Periodicals
In: Journal of Academic Librarianship. - 6 (1980), pp. 16 - 19

MURFIN, MARJORIE E.: National Reference Measurement: What Can It Tell Us about Staffing?
In: College and Research Libraries. - 44 (1983), pp. 321 - 333

MURPHY, MARCY: Evaluating Library Public Service
In: Journal of Library Administration. - 12 (1990), pp. 63 - 90

MYERS, M. J.; J. M. JIRJEES: The Accuracy of Telephone Reference/Information Services in Academic Libraries. - Metuchen, N.J.: Scarecrow Press, 1983

NEL, PIETER J.; HENNIE S. LEROUX: Productivity Measurement in an Information Service with the Aid of the Objective Matrix
In: FID News Bulletin. - 42 (1992), pp. 14 - 18

NEWHOUSE, ROBERT C.: A Library Essential: Needs Assessment
In: Library Review. - 39 (1990), pp. 33 - 36

NILES, JUDITH: Strategies for Assessing and Improving Collection Effectiveness: A Report of the ARL Collection Evaluation Institute, Washington, DC, March 11 - 15, 1991
In: Library Acquisitions: Practice and Theory. - 16 (1992), pp. 57 - 59

Selected Bibliography

NIMMER, RONALD J.: Circulation and Collection Patterns at the Ohio State University Libraries 1973-1977
In: Library Acquisitions: Practice and Theory. - 4 (1980), pp. 61 - 70

NISONGER, THOMAS E.: Collection Evaluation in Academic Libraires: A Literature Guide and Annotated Bibliography. - Englewood, Col.: Libraries Unlimited, 1992

NISONGER, THOMAS E.: An In-depth Collection Evaluation at the University of Manitoba Library: A Test of the Lopez Method
In: Library Resources and Technical Services. - 24 (1980), pp. 329 - 338

NKEREUWEM, E.E.; U. ETENG:
The Application of Operations Research in Library Management: A Case Study of In-library Book Use.
In: Library Review, 43 (1994), pp. 37 - 43

OBERHOFER, CECILIA A.: Disponibilidade de documentos: un modelo de avliacao da satisfacao da demanda em bibliotecas universitarias
In: Ciencia da Informacao. - 10 (1981), pp. 47 - 58

OLAUSSON, CARIN: Evaluation in University Libraries: A Tool for Development
In: Libri. - 42 (1992), pp. 63 - 74

OLSON, EDWIN E.; EDWARD S. WARNER; VERN PINGS; ELAINE SLOANE: Relative Use Patterns of Libraries Serving Medical School Populations
In: Information in the Health Sciences Working to the Future / Ed. by Robert G. Cheshier. - Cleveland: Medical Library Association, 1972, pp.95 - 112

OLSON, L. M.: Reference Service Evaluation in Medium-sized Academic Libraries: A Model
In: Journal of Academic Librarianship. - 9 (1984), pp. 322 - 329

OMVLEE, JENNY: De 'klant op afstand' nader bekeken: Gebruikersonderzoek bij de Bibliotheek van de TU Delft
In: Open. - 25 (1993), 273 - 277

O'NEILL, ANN L.: Evaluating the Success of Acquisitions Departments: A Literature Review
In: Library Acquisitions: Practice and Theory. - 16 (1992), pp. 209 - 219

ONONOGBO, R. U.: User Satisfaction in a Depressed Economy
In: International Library Review. - 21 (1989), pp. 209 - 221

OPACS AND THE USER: Proceedings of the Third Anglo-Nordic Seminar, 8-11 april 1990. - Esbo: NORDINFO, 1991. - (NORDINFO-publications; 19)

ORR, RICHARD H.: Development of Methodologic Tools for Planning and Managing Library Services: II. Measuring a Library's Capability for Providing Documents
In: Bulletin of the Medical Library Association. - 56 (1968), pp. 241 - 267

ORR, RICHARD H.; ARTHUR P. SCHLESS: Document Delivery Capabilities of Major Biomedical Libraries in 1968: Results of a National Survey Employing Standardized Tests
In: Bulletin of the Medical Library Association. - 60 (1972), pp. 382 - 422

ORR, RICHARD H.: Measuring the Goodness of Library Services: A General Framework for Considering Quantitative Measures
In: Journal of Documentation. - 29 (1973), pp. 315 - 332

OSBURN, CHARLES B.: Collection Evaluation and Acquisitions Budgets: A Kaleidoscope in the Making
In: Journal of Library Administration. - 17 (1992). p. 3 - 11

OVERTON, C. M.: Review of Management Information from Computer-Based Circulation Systems in Academic Libraries. - London: The British Library, 1979

PAGE, MARY; MELINDA ANN REAGOR: Library Processing Practices by Discipline: Are Some Books More Equal than Others?
In: Library Resources and Technical Services. - 38 (1994), pp. 161 - 167

PALM, MIRIAM; VICKY REICH: Evaluation under the Gun: Not Necessarily Inferior
In: Acquisitions Librarian. - 6 (1991), pp. 105 - 114

PARK, TAEMIN KIM: The Nature of Relevance in Information Retrieval : An Empirical Study
In: Library Quarterly. - 63 (1993), pp. 318 - 351

PASKOFF, BETH M.: Accuracy of Telephone Reference Service in Health Sciences Libraries
In: Bulletin of the Medical Library Association. - 79 (1991), pp. 182 - 188

PEARSON, RICHARD C.: How Well is Your Library Doing What it Claims to Be Doing?
In: Idaho Librarian. - 45 (1993), pp. 74 - 75

PEASGOOD, ADRIAN N.: Towards Demand-led Book Acquisitions? Experiences in the University of Sussex Library
In: Journal of Librarianship. - 18 (1986), pp. 242 - 256

PEAT, W. L.: The Use of Research Libraries: A Comment about the Pittsburgh Study and Its Critics
In: Journal of Academic Librarianship. - 7 (1981), pp. 229 - 231

PENDLEBURY, J.M.; A.N. PEASGOOD; R.C. YOUNG: Use of Monograph Bookstock in the University of Sussex Library for Teaching and/or for Research: An Analysis based on Loan Records 1981-1991
In: British Journal of Academic Librarianship. - 9 (1994), pp. 127 - 144

PENNER, R. J.: Measuring a Library's Capability
In: Journal of Education for Librarianship. - 13 (1972), pp. 17 - 30

PERFORMANCE MEASURES: A Bibliography / Ed. by Patricia Layzell Ward. - Loughborough: Centre for Library and Information Management and Public Libraries Research Group, 1982. - (Loughborough University of Technology. Centre for Library and Information Management. Reports ; 13)

PETERS, THOMAS: The History and Development of Transaction Log Analysis
In: Library Hi Tech. - 11 (1993), pp. 41 - 67

PETERS, THOMAS; MARTIN KURTH; PATRICIA FLAHERTY; BETH SANDORE; NEAL K. KASKE: An Introduction to the Special Section on Transaction Log Analysis
In: Library Hi Tech. - 11 (1993), pp. 38 - 40

PHILLIPS, SHARON A.: Productivity Measurement in Hospital Libraries: A Case Report
In: Bulletin of the Medical Library Association. - 78 (1990), pp. 146 - 153

PHILIPPS, STEVE: Evaluation. - Lanham, MD: UNIPUB, 1993

PIZER, I. H.; A. M. CAIN: Objective Tests of Library Performance
In: Special Libraries. - 59 (1968), pp. 704 - 711

POLL, ROSWITHA: Guidelines for Performance Measurement - Evaluation of the Draft of the IFLA Manual
In: Quality Issues in the Library and Information Services: Proceedings of a Conference Organised by NORD-INFO and the British Library (Research and Development Department). Held at Hässelby Slott, Stockholm, Sweden, 8-10 October 1993. - Esbo: NORDINFO, 1994, pp. 123 - 129

Selected Bibliography

POLL, ROSWITHA: Leistungsmessung in wissenschaftlichen Bibliotheken
In: Zeitschrift für Bibliothekswesen und Bibliographie. - 39 (1992), pp. 95 - 109

POLL, ROSWITHA: Problems of Performance Evaluation in Academic Libraries
In: INSPEL. - 25 (1991), pp. 24 - 36

POLL, ROSWITHA: Quality and Performance Measurement - A German View
In: British Journal of Academic Librarianship. - 8 (1993), pp. 35 - 47

PORS, NIELS O.: Performance Measurement in the Danish Libraries
In: International Federation of Library Associations and Institutions, 56th IFLA General Conference Stockholm, Sweden 18-24 August 1990, Booklet 1: Division of General Research Libraries. - Den Haag: IFLA, 1990, pp. 35 - 36

POSNETT, N. W.: Introduction of Performance Indicators at the Institute of Development Studies
In: Journal of Information Science. - 19 (1993), pp. 377 - 387

POWELL, R. R.: Reference Effectiveness: A Review of Research
In: Library and Information Science Research. - 6 (1984), pp. 3 - 19

POWELL, RONALD R.: Impact Assessment of University Libraries
In: Encyclopedia of Library and Information Science / Ed. Allen Kent. - Vol. 55, Suppl. 18. - New York: Dekker, 1995, pp. 151 - 161

POWELL, RONALD R.: Impact Assessment of University Libraries: A Consideration of Issues and Research Methodologies
In: Library and Information Science Research. - 14 (1992), pp. 245 - 257

POWER, C. J.; G. H. BELL: Automated Circulation, Patron Satisfaction, and Collection Evaluation in Academic Libraries: A Circulation Analysis Formula
In: Journal of Library Automation. - 11 (1978), pp. 366 - 369

PRELIMINARY RESULTS OF THE INSTITUTIONAL STUDENT SATISFACTION SURVEY, MARCH 1995: EVALUATION AND FEEDBACK / Liverpool John Moores University. - Liverpool: John Moores University, June 1995.

PRITCHARD, SARAH M.: Determining Quality in Academic Libraries
In: Library Trends. - 44 (1996), pp. 572 - 594

PROCEEDINGS OF THE 1ST INTERNATIONAL CONFERENCE ON PERFORMANCE MEASUREMENT IN LIBRARIES AND INFORMATION SERVICES HELD AT LONGHIRST MANAGMENT AND TRAINING CENTRE, LONGHIRST HALL, NORTHUMBERLAND, ENGLAND, 31 AUGUST TO 4 SEPTEMBER 1995 / Editor Pat Wressell. - Newcastle upon Tyne: Information North, 1995

PRYTHERCH, RAY: Evaluation of Services: A Literary Review
In: Outlook on Research Libraries. - 9 (1987), pp. 10 - 12

QUINN, B.: Beyond Efficacy: The Exemplar Librarian as a New Approach to Reference Evaluation
In: Illinois Library. - 76 (1994), pp. 163 - 173

RAFFEL, J. A.; R. SHISHKO: Systematic Analysis of University Libraries. - Cambridge, Mass.: MIT Press, 1969

RALLI, TONY: Performance Measures for Academic Libraries
In: Australian Academic and Research Libraries. - 18 (1987), pp. 1 - 9

RAMSING, KENNETH D.; JON R. WISH: What Do Library Users Want?: A Conjoint Measurement Technique May Yield the Answer
In: Information Processing and Management. - 18 (1982), pp. 237 - 242

RASHID, HASEEB F.: Book Availability as a Performance Measure of a Library: An Analysis of the Effectiveness of a Health Science Library
In: Journal of the American Society for Information Science. - 41 (1990), pp. 501 - 507

REDFERN, MARGARET: Giving an Account: Performance Indicators for Libraries
In: Library Review. - 39 (1990), pp. 7 - 9

REGAZZI, JOHN J.; RODNEY M. HERSBERGER: Queues and Reference Service: Some Implications for Staffing
In: College and Research Libraries. - 39 (1978), pp. 293 - 298

REVILL, DON H.: 'Availability' as a Performance Measure for Academic Libraries
In: Journal of Librarianship. - 19 (1987), pp. 14 - 30

REVILL, DON H.: Performance Assessment in Academic Libraries
In: Do We Really Need Libraries?: Proceedings of the First Joint Library Association Cranfield Institute of Technology Conference on Performance Assessment / Ed. by John Blagden. - Cranfield, 1983, pp. 47 - 55

REVILL, DON H.: Performance Measures for Academic Libraries
In: Encyclopedia of Library and Information Science / Ed. by Allen Kent. - Vol. 45, Suppl. 10. - New York: Dekker, 1990, pp. 294 - 333

REVILL, DON H.: Some Examples and Types of Performance Measures
In: Do We Really Need Libraries?: Proceedings of the First Joint Library Association Cranfield Institute of Technology Conference on Performance Assessment / Ed. by John Blagden. - Cranfield, 1983, pp. 59 - 66

RICHARD, STEPHEN: Library Use of Performance Indicators
In: Library Review. - 41 (1992), pp. 22 - 36

RIDDICK, JOHN F.: Collection Development for the Nineties: A Context for Evaluation
In: Acquisitions Librarian. - 6 (1991), pp. 35 - 43

ROBERTS, STEPHEN A.: Cost Management for Library and Information Science. - London: Butterworth, 1985

RODGER, E. J.; J. GOODWIN: Reference Accuracy at the Fairfax County Public Library. - Washington, D.C.: Metropolitan Washington Library Council, 1984

RODGER, ELIZABETH M.: The Evaluation of Library and Information Services in Times of Economic Restraint: The University View
In: ASLIB Proceedings. - 39 (1987), pp. 349 - 354

ROTHSTEIN, SAMUEL: The Hidden Agenda in the Measurement and Evaluation of Reference Service, or, How to Make a Case for Yourself
In: The Reference Librarian. - 25/26 (1989), pp. 351 - 358

ROTHSTEIN, SAMUEL: The Measurement and Evaluation of Reference Service
In: Library Trends. - 12 (1964), pp. 456 - 472

ROUSE, WILLIAM B.: Optimal Selection of Acquisition Sources
In: Journal of the American Society for Information Science. - 25 (1974), pp. 227 - 231

ROUT, R.K.: Measuring User Satisfaction: A Quantitative Model
In: Indian Association of Special Libraries and Information Centres (IASLIC) Bulletin. - 27 (1982), pp. 1 - 8

RUBIN, RICHARD: In-House Use of Materials in Public Libraries. - Urbana, Ill.: Graduate School of Library and Information Science, 1986. - (Graduate School of Library and Information Science University of Illinois at Urbana-Champaign ; Monograph 18)

RUHIG-DUMONT, ROSEMARY: A Conceptual Basis for Library Effectiveness
In: College and Research Libraries. - 41 (1980), pp. 103 - 111

RUSSEL, ANNE; MICHAEL SHOOLBRED: Developing an Effective Questionnaire
In: Library and Information Research News. - 19 (1995), pp. 28 - 33

RZASA, PHILIP V.; NORMAN R. BAKER: Measures of Effectiveness for a University Library
In: Journal of the American Society for Information Science. - 23 (1972), pp. 248 - 253

SANDISON, A.: The Use of Older Literature and its Obsolescence
In: Journal of Documentation. - 27 (1971), pp. 184 - 199

SANDORE, BETH; PETERS, THOMAS; MARTIN KURTH; PATRICIA FLAHERTY; NEAL K. KASKE: A Manifesto: Regarding the Future of Transaction Log Analysis
In: Library Hi Tech. - 11 (1993), pp. 105 - 106

SANDORE, BETH: Online Searching: What Measure Satisfaction?
In: Library and Information Science Research. - 12 (1990), pp. 33-54

SARACEVIC, T.: Causes and Dynamics of User Frustration in an Academic Library
In: College and Research Libraries. - 38 (1977), pp. 7 - 18

SARGENT, S. H.: The Uses and Limitations of Trueswell
In: College and Research Libraries. - 40 (1979), pp. 416 - 423

SAVARD, R.; P. DELOBEL; J. PANNETON: L'Étude des Clientèles, un Outil pour la Gestion: Le Cas de la Bibliothèque centrale de Montreal
In: Argus. - 23 (1994), pp. 11 - 19

SCHAFFNER, ANN C.; MARIANNE BURLE; JUTTA REED-SCOTT: Automated Collection Analysis: The Boston Library Consortium Experience
In: Advances in Library Resource Sharing. - 3 (1992), pp. 35 - 49

SCHAUER, B. P.: The Economics of Managing Library Service. - Chicago: American Library Association, 1986

SCHLICHTER, DORIS J.; J. MICHAEL PAMBERTON: The Emperor's New Clothes?: Problems of the User Survey as a Planning Tool in Academic Libraries
In: College and Research Libraries. - 53 (1992), pp. 257 - 265

SCHMIDT, JANINE: Practical Experience of Performance Measurement at the State Library of New South Wales
In: Australian Academic and Research Libraries. - 21 (1990), pp. 65 - 77

SCHMIDT, JANINE: Reference Performance in College Libraries
In: Australian Academic and Research Libraries. - 11 (1980), pp. 87 - 95

SCHMIDT, KAREN A.: Lives of Noisy Desperation: A Year's Work in Collection Development, 1989
In: Library Resources and Technical Services. - 34 (1990), pp. 433 - 436

SCHOFIELD, J. L.: Evaluation of an Academic Library's Stock Effectiveness
In: Journal of Librarianship. - 7 (1975), pp. 207 - 227

SCHRADER, A. M.: Performance Measures for Public Libraries: Refinements in Methodology and Reporting
In: Library Research. - 2 (1980), pp. 129 - 155

SCHUCK, BRIAN R.: Assessing a Library Instruction Program
In: Research Strategies. - 10 (1992), pp. 152 - 160

SCHULTE-NÖLKE, PETER: Das Problem der betrieblichen Leistungsmessung in Bibliotheken: Darstellung und Kritik in der Fachliteratur seit Anfang der 70er Jahre
In: Bibliothek. Forschung und Praxis. - 17 (1993), pp. 7 - 28

SCHWARTZ, DIANE G.; DOTTIE EAKIN: Reference Service Standards, Performance Criteria and Evaluation
In: Journal of Academic Librarianship. - 12 (1986), pp. 4 - 8

SCHWARZ, P.: Demand-adjusted Shelf Availability Parameters: A Second Look
In: College and Research Libraries. - 44 (1983), pp. 210 - 219

SCHWUCHOW, WERNER: Wirtschaftlichkeit von Informationsdienstleistungen
In: DBI-Materialien. - 95 (1990), pp. 81 - 99

SEAY, THOMAS; SHEILA SEAMAN; DAVID COHEN: Measuring and Improving the Quality of Public Services: A Hybrid Approach
In: Library Trends. - 44 (1996), pp. 464 - 490

SELF, JAMES: Reserve Readings and Student Grades: Analysis of a Case Study
In: Library and Information Science Research. - 9 (1987), pp. 29-40

SELTH, JEFF; NANCY KOLLER; PETER BRISCOE: The Use of Books within the Library
In: College and Research Libraries. - 53 (1992), pp. 197 - 205

SEYMOUR, CAROL A.; J. L. SCHOFIELD: Measuring Reader Failure at the Catalogue
In: Library Resources and Technical Services. - 17 (1973), pp. 6 - 24

SEYMOUR, SHARON: Online Public Access Catalog User Studies: A Review of Research Methodologies, March 1986 - November 1989
In: Library and Information Science Research. - 13 (1991), pp. 89 - 102

SHAFA, ZARY M.; GLENDA A. THORNTON; JULIE S. ALEXANDER; KRISTINE L. MURPHY; AUDREY V. VANDERHOOF: Regional Study of Vendor Performance for In-print Monographs
In: Library Acquisitions: Practice and Theory. - 16 (1992), pp. 21 - 29

SHAUGHNESSY, THOMAS W.: Assessing Library Effectiveness
In: Journal of Library Administration. - 12 (1990), pp. 1 - 8

SHEPPARD, MARGARET: Some Thoughts Concerning a Structural Framework for Performance Indicators
In: Australian Academic and Research Libraries. - 4 (1990), pp. 44 - 47

SHERMAN, IRVIN H.: What Makes a Library Well Run?
In: Canadian Library Journal. - 41 (1984), pp. 249 - 252

SHIBANDA, G.: Collection Development as Performance Measurement
In: Library Review. - 43 (1994), pp. 44 - 48

SHROYER, ANDREW: Toward Greater Objectivity: Formal Production Standards for Processing Units in Libraries
In: Library Acquisitions: Practice and Theory. - 16 (1992), pp. 127 - 134

SIGGINS, JACK A.: Job Satisfaction and Performance in a Changing Environment
In: Library Trends. - 41 (1992), pp. 299- 315

SLOTE, S. J.: Weeding Library Collections. - 2nd ed. - Littleton, Col.: Libraries Unlimited, 1982

SMET, EGBERT DE: Evaluation of a Computerised Community Information System through Transaction Analysis and User Survey
In: Libri. - 45 (1995), pp. 36 - 44

SMITH, G. STEVENSON: Managerial Accounting and Changing Models of Administrative Behavior: New Methods for New Models
In: Library Trends. - 38 (1989), pp. 189 - 203

SMITH, LISA L.: Evaluating the Reference Interview: A Theoretical Discussion of the Desirability and Achievability of Evaluation
In: Reference Quarterly. - 31 (1991), pp. 75 - 81

SMITH, R. H.; W. GRANADE: User and Library Failures in an Undergraduate Library
In: College and Research Libraries. - 39 (1978), pp. 467 - 473

SPADINGER, INGEBORG; INGEBORG GEIER: Leistungsvergleich zwischen wissenschaftlichen Bibliotheken
In: Zentralblatt für Bibliothekswesen. - 103 (1989), pp. 224 - 225

SPECHT, J.: Patron Use of an Online Circulation System in Known-item Searching
In: Journal of the American Society for Information Science. - 31 (1980), pp. 335 - 346

SPENCER, C. C.: How to Allocate Personnel Costs of Reference
In: Proceedings of the Symposium on Measurement of Reference / Ed. by. K. Emerson. - Chicago, 1974, pp. 35 - 41

SPENCER, C. C.: Random Time Sampling with Self-observation for Library Cost Studies: Unit Costs of Interlibrary Loans and Photocopies at a Regional Medical Library
In: Journal of the American Society for Information Science. - 22 (1971), pp. 153 - 160

A STANDARD FOR THE UNDERTAKING OF USER SURVEYS IN PUBLIC LIBRARIES IN THE UNITED KINGDOM. MANUAL OF GUIDANCE, VERSION 1.0 / Institute of Public Finance Ltd in association with the Committee on Public Library Statistics. - London, 1995

STANDARDS FOR COLLEGE LIBRARIES: Final Version Approved by the ACRL Board and the ALA Standards Committee, February 1995
In: College and Research Libraries News. - 56 (1995), pp. 245 - 257

STANDARDS FOR UNIVERSITY LIBRARIES: EVALUATION OF PERFORMANCE / Prepared by ACRL University Libraries Section's University Library Standards Review Committee; Kent Hendrickson, Chair. Approved June 1989. - Chicago: Association of College & Research Libraries, 1989

STELK, ROGER E.; F. W. LANCASTER: The Use of Textbooks in Evaluating the Collection of an Undergraduate Library
In: Library Acquisitions: Practice and Theory. - 14 (1990), pp. 191 -193

STEYNBERG, SUSAN: Availability and Accessibility as Parameters in Measuring the Document Delivery Capability of an Academic Library
In: Suid-Afrikaanse Tydskrif vir Biblioteek- en Inligtingkunde. - 57 (1989), pp. 372 - 377

STOKLEY, SANDRA L.; MARION T. REID: A Study of Performance of Five Book Dealers Used by Louisiana State University Library
In: Library Resources and Technical Services. - 22 (1978), pp. 117 - 125

STUART, IAN: Some Effects on Library Users of the Delays in Supplying Publications
In: ASLIB Proceedings. - 29 (1977), pp. 35 - 45

STUEART, ROBERT D.; MAUREEN SULLIVAN: Performance Analysis and Appraisal: A How-to-do-it Manual for Librarians. - New York: Neal-Schuman, 1991

SU, LOUISE: An Investigation to Find Appropriate Measures for Evaluating Interactive Information Retrieval
In: ASIS'89. Managing Information and Technology. Proceedings of the 52nd Annual Meeting of the American Society for Information Science, 26, Washington D.C., 30 October - 2 November 1989 / Ed. by Jeffrey Katzer and Gregory B. Newby. - Medford, N.J.: Learned Information, 1989, pp. 13 - 23

SWART, J. H. DE: Is meten weten?
In: Open. - 24 (1992), pp. 82 - 85

TAGLIACOZZO, R.; M. KOCHEN: Information-seeking Behavior of Catalog Users
In: Information Storage and Retrieval. - 6 (1970), pp. 363 - 381

TAGUE, JEAN; ISOLA AJIFERUKE: The Markov Model and the Mixed-poisson Models of Library Circulation Compared
In: Journal of Documentation. - 43 (1987), pp. 212 - 235

TAGUE-SUTCLIFFE, JEAN: Measuring Information: An Information Services Perspective. - San Diego: Academic Press, 1995

THORNE, ROSEMARY; JO BELL WHITLATCH: Patron Online Catalog Success
In: College and Research Libraries. - 55 (1994), pp. 479 - 497

TIEFEL, VIRGINIA: Output or Performance Measures: The Making of a Manual
In: College and Research Libraries News. - 50 (1989), pp. 475 - 478

TILLOTSON, JOY: Is Keyword Searching the Answer
In: College and Research Libraries. - 56 (1995), pp. 199 - 206

TJARKS, LARRY: Evaluating Literature Collections
In: RQ. - 12 (1972), pp. 183 - 185

TJOUMAS, RENEE; VIRGIL L. BLAKE: Counteracting the Divergence between Professional Accreditation and the Evaluation of Library Science Collections
In: Collection Management. - 12 (1990), pp. 43 - 59

TJOUMAS, RENEE; ESTHER E. HORNE: Collection Evaluation: Practices and Methods in Libraries of ALA Accredited Graduate Library Education Programs
In: Advances in Library Administration and Organization. - 5 (1986), pp. 109 - 138

TOBIN, J. C.: A Study of Library "Use Studies"
In: Information Storage and Retrieval. - 10 (1974), pp. 101 - 113

167

TÖRNGREN, MARGARETA: Case Study at Stockholm University Library (RUT)
In: Quality Issues in the Library and Information Services: Proceedings of a Conference Organised by NORD-INFO and the British Library (Research and Development Department). Held at Hässelby Slott, Stockholm, Sweden, 8-10 October 1993. - Esbo: NORDINFO, 1994, pp. 107 - 119

TOPPING, PHIL: The Methodological Problems of Assessing Library Performance
In: Do We Really Need Libraries?: Proceedings of the First Joint Library Association Cranfield Institute of Technology Conference on Performance Assessment / Ed. by John Blagden. - Cranfield, 1983, pp. 13 - 19

TREADWELL, JANE; CHARLES SPORNICK: Translating the Conspectus: Presenting Collection Evaluation Results to Administrators
In: Acquisitions Librarian. - 6 (1991), pp. 45 - 59

TRUESWELL, RICHARD W.: A Quantitative Measure of User Circulation Requirements and Its Possible Effect on Stack Thinning and Multiple Copy Determination
In: American Documentation. - 16 (1965), pp. 20 - 25

TRUESWELL, RICHARD W.: Determining the Optimal Number of Volumes of a Library's Core Collection
In: Libri. - 16 (1966), pp. 49 - 60

TRUESWELL, RICHARD W.: Some Behavioral Patterns of Library Users: the 80/20 Rule
In: Wilson Library Bulletin. - 43 (1969), pp. 459 - 461

TRUESWELL, RICHARD W.: Two Characteristics of Circulation and Their Effect on the Implementation of Mechanized Circulation Control Systems
In: College and Research Libraries. - 25 (1964), pp. 285 - 291

TRUESWELL, RICHARD W.: User Circulation Satisfaction vs. Size of Holdings at Three Academic Libraries
In: College and Research Libraries. - 30 (1969), pp. 204 - 213

TRUETT, CAROL: Weeding and Evaluating the Reference Collection: A Study of Policies and Practices in Academic and Public Libraries
In: Reference Librarian. - 29 (1990), pp. 53 - 68

UNIVERSITY LIBRARY EFFECTIVENESS: A Case Study of the Perceived Outcomes of Structural Change. - Madison: University of Wisconsin, 1990

URQUHART, J. A.; J. L. SCHOFIELD: Measuring Readers' Failure at the Shelf in Three University Libraries
In: Journal of Documentation. - 28 (1972), pp. 233 - 241

VANHouse, Nancy A.; Thomas Childers: Dimensions of Public Library Effectiveness 2: Library Performance
In: Library and Information Science Research. - 12 (1990), pp. 131 - 153

VANHOUSE, NANCY A. : Output Measures in Libraries
In: Library Trends. - 38 (1989), pp. 268 - 279

VINCELETTE, JOYCE P.; FRED C. PFISTER: Improving Performance Appraisal in Libraries
In: Library and Information Science Research. - 6 (1984), pp. 191 - 203

VOKAC, LIBENA: Hodniceni knihoven anebo jak funguje vase knihovna?
In: I'94 Casopis. - 36 (1994), pp. 280, 285 - 286

VOORBIJ, HENK: Availability studies: opzet, nut en beperkingen
In: Open. - 20 (1988), pp. 200 - 204

VOORBIJ, HENK: Collectie-evaluatie volgens een trechtermodel: Een onderzoek naar de tidschriftencollectie van de Koninklijke Bibliotheek
In: Open. - 24 (1992), pp. 420 - 424

WAINWRIGHT, ERIC J.: Collection Adequacy: Meaningless Concept or Measurable Goal?
In: Collection Management in Academic Libraries: Papers Delivered at a National Seminar, Surfers Paradise, Queensland, 16th - 17th February 1984 / Ed. by Cathryn Crowe, Philip Kent and Barbara Paton. - Sydney: Library Association of Australia, University and College Libraries Section, 1984, pp. 1 - 10

WALDHART, THOMAS J.: Performance Evaluation of Interlibrary Loan in the United States: A Review of Research
In: Library and Information Science Research. - 7 (1985), pp. 313 - 331

WALDHART, THOMAS J.; THOMAS P. MARCUM: Productivity Measurement in Academic Libraries
In: Advances in Librarianship. - 6 (1976), pp. 53 - 78

WALL, T.: A Comparative Approach to Assessing the Performance of a Short-loan Collection.
In: Journal of Librarianship and Information Science. - 26 (1994), pp. 193 - 200

WALLACE, LINDA K.: Customer Feedback - How to Get It
In: College and Research Libraries News. - 55 (1994), pp. 64 - 65

WALLACE, PATRICIA M.: How Do Patrons Search the Online Catalog When No One's Looking?: Transaction Log Analysis and Implications for Bibliographic Instruction and System Design
In: RQ. - 33 (1993), pp. 239 - 252

WATSON, RICHARD T.; LEYLAND F. PITT; CHRIS J. CUNNINGHAM; DEON NEL: User Satisfaction and Service Quality of the IS Department: Closing the Gaps
In: Journal of Information Technology. - 8 (1993), pp. 257 - 265

WEECH, T. L.; HERBERT GOLDHOR: Obtrusive versus Unobtrusive Evaluation of Reference Service in Five Illinois Public Libraries: A Pilot Study
In: Library Quarterly. - 52 (1982), pp. 305 - 324

WEEDING OF COLLECTIONS IN SCI-TECH-LIBRARIES / Ed. by E. Mount. - New York: Haworth Press, 1986

WELLS, J.: The Influence of Library Usage on Undergraduate Academic Success
In: Australian Academic and Research Libraries. - 26 (1995), pp. 121-128

WENGER, CHARLES B.; CHRISTINE B. SWEET; HELEN J. STILES: Monograph Evaluation for Acquisitions in a Large Research Library
In: Journal of the American Society for Information Science. - 30 (1979), pp. 88 - 92

WESSEL, C. J.: Criteria for Evaluating Technical Library Effectiveness
In: ASLIB Proceedings. - 20 (1968), pp. 455 - 481

WHITE, G. T.: Quantitative Measures of Library Effectiveness
In: Journal of Academic Librarianship. - 3 (1977), pp. 128 - 136

WHITE, HERBERT S.: Cost Benefit Analysis & Other Fun & Games
In: Library Journal. - 110 (1985), pp. 118 - 121

WHITLATCH, J. B.; K. KIEFFER: Service at San Jose State University: Survey of Document Availability
In: Journal of Academic Librarianship. - 4 (1978), pp. 196 - 199

WIDDOWS, RICHARD; TRIA A. HENSLER; MARLAYA H. WYNCOTT: The Focus Group Interview: A Method for Assessing Users' Evaluation of Library Service
In: College and Research Libraries. - 52 (1991), pp. 352 - 359

WIEMERS, EUGENE JR.; CAROL ANN BALDWIN; BARBARA KAUTZ; JEAN ALBRECHT; LINDA HAACK LOMKER: Collection Evaluation: A Practical Guide to the Literature
In: Library Acquisitions: Practice and Theory. - 8 (1984), pp. 65 - 76

WILDEMUTH, BARBARA M.; ANN L. O'NEILL: The "Known" in Known-Item Searches: Empirical Support for User-Centred Design
In: College and Research Libraries. - 56 (1995), pp. 265 - 281

WILLEMSE, JOHN: Improving Interlending through Goal Setting and Performance Measurement
In: Interlending and Document Supply. - 21 (1993), pp. 13 - 17

WILLEMSE, JOHN: Stygings in tydskrifsubskripsies en beskikbaarheid in universiteitsbiblioteke
In: South African Journal of Library and Information Science. - 59 (1991), pp. 135 - 142

WILLEMSE, JOHN: Summary of the Paris Workshop 1989 on Performance Measurement
In: IFLA Journal. - 16 (1990), pp. 458 - 462

WILLIAMS, DELMUS E.: Evaluation and the Process of Change in Academic Libraries
In: Advances in Library Administration and Organisation. Vol. II / Ed. by G. McCabe and B. Kreissman. - Greenwich: Jai Press, 1983, pp. 151 - 174

WILLIAMS, R.: An Unobtrusive Survey of Academic Library Reference Services
In: Library and Information Research News. - 10 (1987), pp. 12 - 40

WILLIAMS, ROBERT V.: Productivity Measurements in Special Libraries: Prospects and Problems for Use in Performance Evaluation
In: Special Libraries. - 79 (1988), pp. 101 - 114

WINKWORTH, IAN: Into the House of Mirrors: Performance Measurement in Academic Libraries
In: British Journal of Academic Librarianship. - 8 (1993), pp. 17 - 33

WINKWORTH, IAN: Performance Indicators for Polytechnic Libraries
In: Library Review. - 39 (1990), pp. 23 - 41

WINKWORTH, IAN: Performance Measurement and Performance Indicators
In: Collection Management in Academic Libraries / Ed. by Clare Jenkins and Mary Moreley. - Aldershof: Gower, 1991, pp. 57 - 93

WITTKOPF, BARBARA; CRUSE, PATRICIA: Using the ACRL Performance Manual: The LSU Libraries
In: College and Research Libraries News. - 52 (1991), pp. 571 - 572

WONG, S. K. M.; Y. Y. YAO; G. SALTON; C. BUCKLEY: Evaluation of an Adaptive Linear Model
In: Journal of the American Society for Information Science. - 42 (1991), pp. 723 - 730

WOOD, FIONA: Evaluation of a University Library's Catalogue: Patron Usage, Problems and Policy Direction. - Canberra: Australian National University, 1984. - (ANU Library Occasional Paper ; 4)

WORTMAN, WILLIAM A.: Collection Management: Background and Principles. - Chicago, London: American Library Association, 1989

YOURKOV, S. V.: End Result of Library Activities as a Variable of All Round Analysis of Public Library Functioning
In: Journal of Library and Information Science. - 15 (1990), pp. 51 - 61

ZWEIZIG, DOUGLAS L.: So Go Figure: Measuring Library Effectiveness
In: Public Libraries. - 26 (1987), pp. 21 - 24

ZWEIZIG, DOUGLAS L.: Measuring Library Use
In: Drexel Library Quaterly. - 13 (1977), pp. 3 - 15

IFLA Publications 1995/96

☐ **No. 71: The Image of the Library and Information Profession**
How we see Ourselves: An Investigation
Edited by Russell Bowden
and Donald Wijasuriya
1995. 86 Pages. HB. DM 68.00
For IFLA members: DM 51.00
ISBN 3-598-21798-6

☐ **No. 72/73: World Guide to Library Archive and Information Science Education**
Edited by Josephine Riss-Fang, Robert D. Stueart, and Kulthida Tuamsuk
2nd rev. and enl. edition 1995
XIII, 585 Pages. HB. DM 168.00
For IFLA members: DM 126.00
ISBN 3-598-21799-4

☐ **No. 74: Bibliotecas de arte, arquitectura y diseño**
Perspectivas actuales
Art, Architecture and Design Libraries Current Trends
1995. II, 441 Pages. HB. DM 168.00
For IFLA members: DM 126.00
ISBN 3-598-21801-X

☐ **No. 75: Multilingual Glossary for Art Librarians**
English with Indexes in Dutch, French, German, Italian, Spanish and Swedish
Edited by IFLA Section of Art Libraries
2nd rev. and enl. edition 1996
V, 183 Pages. HB. DM 98.00
For IFLA members: DM 73.50
ISBN 3-598-21802-8

K·G Saur Verlag München · New Providence · London · Paris
A Reed Reference Publishing Company
Postfach 70 16 20 · D-81316 München
Tel. (089) 7 69 02-0 · Fax (089) 7 69 02-150
E-mail-address: 100730,1341@compuserve.com